Bound *for the* Promised Land

HAYA BENHAYIM WITH MENAHEM BENHAYIM

Purple Pomegranate Productions
84 Page Street
San Francisco, CA 94102

On Jordan's stormy banks I stand
And cast a wishful eye
To Canaan's fair and happy land,
Where my possessions lie.

I am bound for the Promised Land,
I am bound for the Promised Land.
O who will come and go with me?
I am bound for the Promised Land.

©2004, Purple Pomegranate Productions
Cover design by David Yapp

For more information write to:
    Reprint Permissions
    Purple Pomegranate Productions
    84 Page Street, San Francisco, CA 94102

07 06 05   10 9 8 7 6 5 4 3

Benhayim, Menahem
Haya Benhayim with Menahem Benhayim—2nd ed.
Library of Congress Cataloging–Publication Data
Bound for the Promised Land
        p.   cm.
ISBN: 1-881022-15-3 (pbk.)

1 Bible. 2. Jews. 3. Jesus (Y'shua). 4. Hope. 5. Israel.
                                                        CIP

All Scripture quoted, unless otherwise noted, is from the
Holy Bible, Revised Standard Version.

Purple Pomegranate Productions is a division of Jews for Jesus®

TABLE OF CONTENTS

FOREWORD

Haya and Menahem Benhayim were the first Messianic
Jewish couple to make *aliyah* (immigrate to Israel) from the
United States of America. Their story is told from Haya's
perspective. My wife Martha and I have been privileged to
know them since 1977, two years before we ourselves made
aliyah, and earlier this year we were present at the
celebration of the fortieth anniversary of their *aliyah*. I can
safely say that the Benhayims are beloved by the entire Body
of Messiah in Israel. They are pioneers, and they deserve our
appreciation as those who went before and paved the way.
Haya gives us tableaux of "what it was like in those days." We
hope that this narrative—in some ways an idyll like the
biblical books of Ruth and Philemon—will encourage other
Messianic Jews to leave the Diaspora, make *aliyah* and find
their place in Israel, the Land God has given to the Jewish
People.

—David H. Stern

Preface

This is the story of Haya Benhayim, the seventh child of
Jewish immigrants who moved from East Europe to America
in the early decades of the twentieth century. It describes
Haya's struggle to find her place in the family circle, her
encounter with committed believers in Yeshua, and their
impact on her life, which eventually led to her renewed faith
in the God of her fathers and His long-rejected Messiah. It
depicts how she first met other Messianic believers. One of
these (myself) was destined to become her husband and
companion in her return to the ancient homeland of our
people.

I too, was the seventh child of East European Jewish
immigrants; thus Haya and I encountered many similar
childhood experiences.

—Menahem Benhayim

PROLOGUE

The air was heavy and hot. A thick, drowsy calm engulfed us. Scarcely a sound broke the monotony of the languid Sabbath afternoon. My husband and I were resting in our small apartment facing an empty courtyard. The rows of sleepy blocks of flats behind us formed a jagged square. They too seemed to be wrapped in the hypnotic languor of the day.

It was the afternoon of Yom Kippur, the Day of Atonement, the most solemn and sacred day of the Hebrew calendar. We lived in a frontier town—Eilat—on the edge of the great Negev desert in southern Israel. The streets were virtually deserted. Even our wild and woolly town, which hardly ever paused to mark religious solemnities, was gripped by the spirit of the lonely annual fast day. *"On the tenth day of this seventh month is the day of atonement; it shall be for you a time of holy convocation, and you shall afflict yourselves ..."* (Leviticus 23:27).

Menahem and I normally spent the day at home, punctuated by visits to friends with whom we prayed and read from the Bible. We observed the ancient fast out of a sense of identification with our people and their spiritual yearnings.

In a few hours the sun would set with a lavish display of desert beauty. Fantastic splashes of color and shadow would paint the skies and the hills of Edom overlooking the Red Sea shore. With the dark it would be so much cooler. We would complete our reading of the Book of Jonah. This tale of the ancient Jewish prophet appealed very much to us. In our own way, we too had experienced that same fear, that same urge to flight, and the strange moves of God leading us into unfamiliar territory.

In the evening, the synagogues would again be thronged with worshippers—and the curious and once-a-year visitors. The ancient shofar (ram's horn) would be sounded—one shrill, piercing blast to announce the completion of the day's long ritual. It was said to be a reminder to God of the covenant that He had made with Abraham at Isaac's binding.

> *And Abraham lifted up his eyes and looked, and behold, behind him was a ram, caught in a thicket by his horns; and Abraham went and took the ram, and offered it up as a burnt offering instead of his son ... And the angel of the Lord called to Abraham ... "By myself I have sworn, says the Lord, because you have done this, and have not withheld your son, your only son. I will indeed bless you ... and by your descendants shall all the nations of the earth bless themselves, because you have obeyed my voice" (Genesis 22:13-18).*

My husband stirred from his reveries on the low wooden cot we used as a sofa for afternoon naps. The shrill wailing of the town's warning siren had shattered the unearthly calm of the holy day.

"Wh-a-t's that?"

"It couldn't be an air raid drill; they'd never choose a day like this for a drill," I thought.

"Maybe it's an electrical fault in the system. That has happened before, you know," my husband ventured.

"What a time for an electrical failure!"

The siren's long, anguished screeching continued.

People began to gather in the courtyard—perplexed, worried parents and children, worshippers hurrying home from the nearby synagogues.

Someone suggested, "Let's turn on the radio!"

The more devout protested, "On the Day of Atonement there's no broadcasting. It's forbidden to turn on the radio."

Indeed, the Israel Broadcasting Authority had ceased operating from the afternoon preceding the fast day—as almost every other activity involving Jews also stopped.

The siren continued to wail. Someone brought out a transistor radio and turned it on. We were surprised to hear patriotic Israeli music being played.

"Something is up," someone commented nervously. "They wouldn't have music like this playing on Yom Kippur. There must be some important news coming."

The anxious discussion was interrupted by the bellowing of a loudspeaker truck passing slowly through the town's streets: "Citizens of Eilat. This is a genuine alarm. This is not a drill. Go to the shelter nearest you at once. I repeat, this is a genuine alarm. This is not a drill. Go to the nearest shelter at once."

My husband and I acted as wardens for the shelter in the courtyard behind our flat. It was a large underground bunker that had been built in the wake of terrorist activity against the town. Menahem ran for the keys and we both donned our protective helmets. We opened the large metal door and let people in. The newscast began as we huddled around a small transistor radio.

"The Israel Defense Forces announce that at 1:50 P.M. Syrian and Egyptian forces mounted simultaneous attacks against our forces in the Golan Heights and along the Suez Canal ..."

For the fourth time in modern Israel's 25-year history, a life-and-death struggle for survival was again to be waged. For us, it was our second experience of war since immigrating to Israel from the United States early in 1963.

What had brought us here to take part in the movement of Jewish return to the ancestral homeland? This is a question we have frequently been asked.

Of the estimated five-and-a-half million Jews living in America in 1963, only a few thousand had settled in Israel. Yet this was a movement which overshadowed every other similar event in Israel's long history. It was far greater than its most celebrated counterpart in biblical days, when the Persian ruler Cyrus had permitted his Jewish subjects to return to their homeland. *"Whoever is among you ... let him go up ..."* (Ezra 1:3, 2 Chronicles 36:23). In fact, these encouraging words are the very last words of the original Hebrew Scriptures. (Since in Christian Bibles Malachi is the last book of the Old Testament, evangelicals often suppose mistakenly that the Old Testament ends with a curse.)

Nonetheless, in the eyes of many of our people, we were disloyal. They thought we had thrown in our lot with the Gentiles, with those they thought were the mortal enemies of Judaism and the Jewish people. We had dared to declare openly, in the words of Simon bar Yonah, our ancient Jewish kinsman, that Yeshua is the Messiah, the son of the living God (Matthew 16:16). And we were not ashamed to acknowledge him as our king and redeemer.

"Why do you have to accept this goyish (Gentile) religion?" a member of a left-wing communal settlement in Galilee once joshed us in friendly, but earnest admonition.

In this story, I hope to set forth some answers to the whys and wherefores of our journey of reconciliation with Israel's

most illustrious Son, and to trace the steps whereby we were led back to the homeland of the Jewish people during the twentieth century.

Chapter One

WHAT A BEAUTIFUL STAR

Give me your tired, your poor,
Your huddled masses yearning to breathe free,
The wretched refuse of your teeming shore.
Send these, the homeless, tempest-tost, to me,
I lift my lamp beside the golden door!

These words of Emma Lazarus, an American Jewish poetess of the nineteenth century, are taken from her ode to the American refuge entitled "The New Colossus." They are inscribed on the pedestal of the Statue of Liberty in New York harbor.

Countless folk, my parents among them, streamed past the Liberty Torch during the first decades of the twentieth century. They were Jews and Gentiles, educated and uneducated, the ambitious, the persecuted, the misfits and the hopeful. They poured through America's gateway into the *goldena medina*, as the immigrant Jews affectionately dubbed their new homeland, the "golden land."

My father, a restless and energetic young man, soon learned the trade of baking. He settled with his parents, devout Orthodox Jews, in the densely-populated area in and around New York City. There they could be close to the masses of Jewish immigrants, many of whom clung to their ancient traditions.

Father was more or less faithful to these traditions, but he also wanted to accommodate himself to the modern age and to take advantage of all the freedoms the New World offered. One of the adjustments he made in this respect was to choose his own wife, an immigrant from East Europe like himself. Forsaking the long drawn out formalities and arrangements common in the "old country," they decided to elope.

Father was eighteen at the time, Mother a few years older. (How much older was a well-kept secret, which I never learned.) The young couple moved to upstate New York, finally settling down in a beautiful part of southern New England.

Stratford was a quiet town, founded in 1639 by English immigrants from Stratford-on-Avon. They had emigrated to the British colony of Connecticut a generation after their most renowned citizen, William Shakespeare, had passed from the scene.

Nearly three centuries later, in 1925, when my family settled in Stratford, only one or two other Jewish families had found their way there, and there was no synagogue. Life was very different from the strict traditional Jewish environment in which my parents had both been nurtured.

We were three girls and four boys; I was the youngest of seven. In childhood, I seldom met other Jewish children outside of our home. We had to travel to neighboring Bridgeport for any Jewish communal activities. Mother kept a strictly kosher kitchen, and we observed most of the Jewish holidays. We all knew we were Jewish, and in some mysterious way "different," but we still wanted to be "like everyone else."

Learning that I was Jewish, a schoolmate once spat out at me bitterly: "You dirty Jew!" When the teacher heard of the incident, she called the child to the front of the classroom and made her apologize to me. Yet it hurt me to think that just because I was born Jewish, I had to be singled out like that.

I remember a friend of the family suddenly remarking to Mother during the course of a conversation, "You know, I like you—even though you're a Jew." We didn't appreciate that kind of compliment at all!

During my second grade in public school, I met Eunice Berglund, a kind, loving child of Swedish descent. I sensed that she was different from the rest of the class in some way. Her mother Hildur had been a prodigy in biblical subjects. As a child of eight, she had been taken on tours of Europe from her native Sweden to give Bible talks. A few years later, she had been drawn into the great wave of emigration moving across Europe to the United States, where she met and married Gus Berglund, a Swedish building contractor. The couple raised two gifted children, Eunice and Leigh.

While Eunice was in primary school she was taken to have a tonsillectomy. (In those days it was almost a fad to have one's tonsils removed early.) Although the doctors informed the family that failures in such operations were "one in a million," the result was disastrous. A piece of the tonsil was dislodged into Eunice's chest during the surgery and infected her lung. Nothing they could do at the time was sufficient to stem the deterioration in Eunice's health and she was given only a short time to live. The Berglunds lavished their prayers, love and life savings upon the stricken child in order to make her life as radiant as possible during the dark days that followed. In winter, they moved to the sun-filled climate of Florida to avoid the harsh New England cold and indeed succeeded in extending Eunice's life span far beyond the medical experts' predictions.

Eunice and I had become chums, but now we were separated for long periods of time. Whenever we could, we visited together, and our two families also became good friends. The Bible was a frequent topic of discussion. Like her mother, Eunice was well-versed in it.

Our family, meanwhile, was prospering materially in the "Golden Land." My twin brothers, Mendy and Charly, teamed up with another brother, Bunny, and opened a quality grocery store in the Stratford Shopping Center. They worked hard and steadily, showing a profit even during the Great Depression.

Charly was the spokesman for the boys. He was articulate and sharp-tempered, and he could rip us to pieces with his acid tongue. He would quarrel vigorously with our sister Sally. At the same time, he possessed great powers of persuasion. He once turned up at an open meeting of the Town Council where some important local issue was under discussion. Everyone seemed to be on one side, but Charly disagreed. He took the floor and presented the other side of the issue so forcefully that he carried the whole meeting along with him in the final vote.

Family life in some ways resembled a hectic public meeting. Before her marriage, Sally was especially aggressive at home. Perhaps she had decided that in our kind of large family setup, with each of us a keen individualist, the best defense was offense. And I, the "kid sister," was often the victim and scapegoat of her highly active "defense mechanism."

My oldest brother, Abe, invested a good deal of his individualism in baseball. In fact, he was sorely tempted to make a career of it. He was the star pitcher on local teams and was actually offered a contract by the Cleveland Indians. Still in his teens, he would have had to be "farmed out" to a

minor league team until he was ready for the "big league."
But Mother strenuously objected to his leaving home. Finally,
he decided to settle for a job with the General Electric
Company in Bridgeport. He remained with the company for
forty-seven years, retiring as an executive in the receiving
department of the Bridgeport branch.

When Abe was thirty, he re-enacted our parents' adventure
in breaking with past tradition—with a vengeance. He
eloped with a co-worker who was Gentile. It was a reprise
of "Abie's Irish Rose," except that Peggy was of Welsh
descent. Once again, the ancient lament of Jewish parents,
reminiscent of the pathetic complaints of Samson's parents,
was heard in a Jewish household! *"Is there not a woman
among the daughters of your kinsmen, or among all our
people, that you must go to take a wife from the
uncircumcised Philistines?"* (Judges 14:3)

Mother and Father were unhappy about the marriage to
the end of their lives. It wasn't that they were prejudiced
against Gentiles. They had excellent relations with their
Gentile neighbors. In fact, Father was quite popular with the
local Irish Catholic police, who affectionately dubbed him
"Kelly." But being traditional Jews, they felt very strongly that
people shouldn't "marry out" of the faith.

I had an excellent rapport with at least one member of
the family, my sister Annie. Olive-skinned, black-eyed, with
beautiful auburn hair, she was stunning—with a gentle and
lovable disposition to match. We developed a strong
friendship. When Annie was eighteen, just out of high
school, an unusual rash appeared on her back. At first she
ignored it, but when it persisted she sought medical aid. The
local doctor treated it quite casually, but it grew worse.
Finally, she was referred to a skin specialist, who diagnosed it

as a rare skin disease called pemphigus.

"Why did you wait so long?" he asked sadly. He explained to our heartbroken family that the chances for Annie's recovery were very slim. For six months, my sister lay in Bridgeport Hospital hopelessly ill. Shortly before she died, she asked that the family be gathered under the window of her room and intone one of the old, melancholy Hebrew chants. It was an incongruous scene, the men standing below her window chanting an old Hebrew melody.

Her death was a bitter blow to us all. I remember the stark, solemn funeral procession. Orthodox Jewish funerals are very somber and plain: No flowers, no music, no elaborate services or requiems—only the plaintive chanting of the cantor or officiating rabbi and the sobbing of the mourners. Even my tough, hard-bitten brother Charly wept like a child.

We were stricken with a succession of family illnesses during those years. A few years following Annie's death, Father developed cancer of the pancreas, which spread through his whole body. It brought him agonizing pain, until his death after two years of horrible suffering. Mother outlived him by only four years, also dying following an extended illness.

I distinctly remember a condolence visit to our home by a rabbi from nearby Bridgeport following Father's death in June 1941. The subject of a Jewish state in the Holy Land came up. The rabbi remarked: "I don't think we'll see it in our lifetime." I couldn't help demurring, "I'm not sure about that prediction." It was only seven years later in May 1948, that the modern State of Israel was founded. I made my own personal return to our ancient homeland fifteen years afterwards. I later learned that this rabbi lived to see the

State and came to Israel, where he died and was buried.

I became quite depressed. What was the use of living? I was desperate. Our family had all the material needs of life, including not a few luxuries—a successful business, a summer cottage on the Housatonic River, a new Cadillac every year. But sickness, family discord and loneliness had emptied all these of meaning. After Father's death, I decided to buy a Bible—one that included the New Testament—and took up the practice of daily reading. Although I found some comfort in this, it existed in a separate compartment of my life.

I was actually the first in the family to own a Bible. Of course we had Orthodox prayer books in the house, but these were quite beyond my understanding and didn't reach me at all.

Moreover, I was a woman; and as far as the popular, old-time Jewish religion was concerned, it wasn't essential for me to have access to sacred literature. Jewish women were expected to be concerned about the "practical" aspects of Judaism—the dietary laws, observing the Sabbath and holiday rites, and finding a suitable Jewish husband! In fact, the traditional practicing Jewish male to this day recites a very revealing blessing each morning: "Blessed art Thou, O Lord . . . that Thou hast not made me a woman."

My older brothers were far from traditional in their daily practice, but they still ruled the roost at home. I had little or nothing to say about the way things should be. After all, what could their little sister know about the essentials of life?

We were the first generation of our family to be born in the "New World." Through our immigrant relatives and friends, we were still nourished by the traditions and lifestyle of a European civilization that was rapidly disintegrating. We heard Yiddish spoken by our parents and their generation, but we refused to speak it. Looking back, we didn't do badly from a purely materialistic perspective. But spiritually we were severely deprived, living in a kind of wasteland.

In Europe, where our family had lived for generations, a terrible Holocaust was brewing. It was to provide a climax of horror for the Jewish people and Western civilization alike. Although it seemed remote from the small-town life we were living, it was bound to affect us.

Then in December 1941 came the attack on Pearl Harbor. America was again involved with the "Old World." The pretense of isolation from that world had to be abandoned. I remember a newsman, a friend of my brothers, speaking to Mendy soon after America's entry into the war.

"How do you feel about getting into the military?" he asked.

"I'll be glad to go," Mendy replied.

The next day, his statement was featured in the local newspaper in a front-page center article under the caption: "Glad to go."

Sure enough, Mendy left with the first contingent of Stratfordians called up after Pearl Harbor. Charly was desolate at this first separation from his twin brother. He followed him into service not long afterwards, but they served in different units until the war's end.

My sister Sally married. She settled with her husband Eli in southern Florida and raised two daughters, Leanne and Glenna.

I heard from Eunice from time to time. Her physical condition was progressively worsening. One warm September day in Florida, her mother was standing by her bedside when she heard her speaking.

"Do I follow that path?" she asked.

Her mother moved closer, trying to understand what was taking place. Then she heard Eunice repeat three times: "What a beautiful star!" Her face became radiant as three times she again exclaimed: "What a beautiful city!" And Eunice slipped into Eternity after eighteen years of suffering and struggle.

Chapter Two

TURNING POINT

The war was over! My brothers were back home. Business was flourishing. Life was back to normal. For six days a week, I worked half days in the store. Then I cleaned the big house and cooked supper for my three bachelor brothers and myself.

In summer, I would join them on weekends at the family cottage by the side of a country road along the shores of the Housatonic River. It was rustic, remote, sometimes even serene. But only on the outside. Inside, I was seething. One year, two years. I had to get away. The drudgery, the emptiness—just to acquire money, comfort and status!

For my brothers—strong-willed, self-sufficient, determined to make good in the American way, as they saw it—that was the purpose of life. It was even more important for them than marriage and raising a family, which might interfere with their drive for success.

But for me, there had to be something more to living. I declared my personal independence—or so I thought. I went off to Florida to visit my sister Sally and her family. I became their babysitter, shared in the housework and did a few stints of commercial work. All the while I was trying to live a modern, swinging life: dates, boyfriends, parties, dances—living it up.

Strangely, I continued to read the Bible faithfully. But my lifestyle didn't seem to relate to my reading. I had yet to have any decisive encounter with the Author of the Book.

Then it happened!

It was a very dark, starless night, pitch black as I lay on my bed in the enclosed porch which was my bedroom in Sally and Eli's home. I had just about reached the limit of my personal, self-centered declaration of independence. I knew that cheap thrills were not the antidote to drudgery, that profligacy didn't fill up one's spiritual coffers any more than money or status. Where was I to turn now?

I felt I was being enveloped in a darkness as thick as the gloomy night around me. For a moment, I had the most eerie sensation of being in an abyss—I was falling deeper, and deeper and deeper.... Was this a vision, a nightmare, *a horror of great darkness* falling upon me as once it had upon Abraham? (Genesis 15:12).

Whatever it was, I was shaken up! Its intensity was so powerful that I cried out in great fear. I sensed a mysterious presence in the room. Surely, I thought, the Lord is dealing with me, convicting me of sin, hell and impending judgment (John 16:8-11). I had been reading the Bible, but till now the message had reached only my head. Now the message was finally filtering down into my heart. And now my daily Bible reading plus the words and prayers of my friend Eunice Berglund and her mother Hildur, were pointing me to Yeshua.

"O God have mercy!" was all I could think of saying. "O God have mercy!" It was the prayer of the tax-gatherer in Yeshua's parable (Luke 18:9-14).

To my utter astonishment and relief, I sensed a clear response to my cry. I felt as though a great burden had literally rolled off my back.

"O God, what must I do now? And what will my sister

and her husband say of my experience? And who shall I go to and speak to?"

I had heard of a small storefront fellowship in Miami Beach from Eunice and her mother, who had suggested I visit the place when in Florida. This casual scrap of information awakened in my memory and took on crucial meaning at this moment in my life. I sought out the fellowship.

Shortly after my nighttime experience, I walked into the meeting place. A bookshelf was lined with Bibles, tracts and other literature. There was a desk, a chair and a room filled with folding chairs for public meetings. A piano and a pulpit stood on the platform. Passages from the Bible, neatly framed, hung along the walls.

I looked about me, pleased at the "un-churchiness" of the atmosphere. There was even something Jewish in its simplicity. A beautiful *menorah* (seven-branched candelabra) rested on the piano. There were no images or crucifixes. I felt comfortable in the room.

Mrs. Lindsay, a widow raised as a Roman Catholic who had later joined the evangelical movement, had founded the fellowship. Her colleague was Edna MacArthur, an older woman who had joined her to reach out to the Jewish people. Southern Florida was an exploding resort center and retirement area. Multitudes of Jews were settling there or came as tourists year after year.

"May I help you, Miss?" one of the ladies greeted me. Smiling a bit nervously, I replied, "Well, I'm Jewish and I'm a believer in Yeshua. I wanted to meet other believers."

"You are? O praise God, my dear! It's so wonderful!"

The ladies sat me down and we conversed for a few minutes. Tactfully and gently, they drew me into the fellowship.

"We're getting ready for a small meeting in a little while," Mrs. Lindsay remarked. "Would you like to join us?"

"Fine," I replied.

When the meeting commenced, we sang the hymn "Sweeter As the Years Go By," which touched me deeply.

I continued to attend the little fellowship and after a while shared some responsibilities with the ladies.

I spoke to Sally about my newfound faith and of my life being transformed. "Well, if it makes you happy, I'm glad for you," Sally commented. "But you can be sure it's not for me. I guess it's good for people who have the worst in life. No, it's not for me. God has been good to me, so I don't see that I need any salvation!"

After a few months, Sally's in-laws learned of my beliefs. They also lived in the Miami area and, like my own parents, were immigrants. Belief in Yeshua as the Messiah of Israel was definitely not part of their pattern of thinking. It was strange, and not a little shocking, for a "nice Jewish girl" to get involved with something like that!

Sally began to press me about my plans. "You know, Haya, my in-laws visit and they also help us out financially. We're not having an easy time of it. Eli isn't doing well, and we can use their help. Couldn't you get married to a nice Jewish boy and settle down?"

At the time, there was no one in the offing. So Sally became more direct. "Wouldn't it be better if you went back to the boys in Connecticut?" she suggested.

At prayer meetings I brought up the touchy situation I now found myself in. The ladies were sympathetic. They thought the answer for me was Bible School. They knew of one in Pennsylvania which they were sure would be suitable for me.

I decided to apply. Meanwhile, I took work in an office as a typist in order to earn money for the journey and for incidentals if I was accepted. In a very short while I received an acceptance notice from the school and told Sally.

The morning of my departure was an emotional time for us. Sally was crying, and one of my little nieces was following me about wondering why her auntie Haya was leaving. Sally hugged me as I left the house and handed me a bag of sliced roast chicken that she had prepared for me for the long journey. I was touched by my sister's gesture. Like all farewells, there was a certain sadness at the parting of our ways and the uncertainty of what lay ahead.

Chapter Three

A WILDERNESS JOURNEY

I was deep in the hill country of western Pennsylvania. Several wooden structures, rather crudely constructed, constituted the Bible School. What a striking contrast to the free and easy stucco-and-villa style of Miami! Nearby, there were forests, farming villages and an air of seclusion. Here I was in the Pennsylvania countryside, far from the sun-and-fun-seeking multitudes who annually flocked to the Florida "fleshpots."

The semester started off with a lively revival at the first chapel meeting of staff and students. A spirit of joy overflowed us during those first two mornings. Song, praise and worship! Testimonies, confession, prayer! The dean suspended the opening classes. Two by two we were sent out into the neighboring villages and the nearest town to bear witness to the joy-giving, soul-saving Redeemer.

And then we returned to normal life, to "business as usual"—perhaps the bane of all revivals, the stumbling-stone that trips up so many believers. How hard to return from the beautiful exalted heights back to the lower plains and marshlands of life! There were rules to be enforced. They were hard and fast and based on inflexible principles: dresses must be worn well below the knees, beckoning gently to the ankles, women's hair must be kept long and worn in a net, no dating the opposite sex except with permission from the staff—and a report on what the couple planned to do had to be presented orally beforehand.

Everyone was assigned a place in the dining room, and the seating arrangement must be adhered to at all meals. I had to sit with a young woman from the area who was convinced that I didn't belong there. The head of the table, one of the staff, was immensely amused by the "cute" rivalry.

Everybody had his own fixed daily chores. Everyone had to seek the "second blessing," the second work of grace. (I had but recently come into the kingdom by grace; what was this work?) I was young, very young in the spiritual life. And I had grown up in a culture so very different from the one prevailing at the school.

One evening, I looked out the window of my room. Three young men were gathered around a thick oak. One of them seemed to be hugging the tree, gripping the old oak with no little feeling. Another had already climbed to the top. In astonishment, I turned to my roommate Hazel, a delightful, friendly and gentle country girl. "What are they doing up that tree?" I asked innocently. Hazel looked out and nonchalantly replied: "O, they're just being blessed."

Frankly, I was too stunned to probe the connection between hugging and climbing trees and "being blessed." But then, a more inspired person than myself once plaintively observed: "Poems are made by fools like me, but only God can make a tree!"

I was actually the only one at the school who came from outside rural Pennsylvania. It must have showed. After a while, I began to feel like the Ruth of Keats' "Ode to a Nightingale" who, "sick for home, stood in tears amid the alien corn."

Early one morning, towards the end of the semester, I began to brood over the situation. It was still dark as I lay in the lower bunk of the double-tiered bed. A wave of despair and loneliness surged through me. I could no longer control my feeling of isolation, and began to weep bitterly. To my surprise, Hazel, who normally would have been out of the room early to attend to her early morning chores, was still in bed. She jumped down and stood beside me. Very tenderly, in her sweet country accent, she asked: "Is there anything I can do for you?" "No, Hazel," I sobbed back softly. "I don't think there is. I just don't seem to fit in here."

I was still in touch with my brothers. When I wrote them that I was interested in returning to Connecticut at the end of the semester, they mailed me a check to cover the bus fare home. It had been some three years since I had last seen them. I must confess I was returning with no little trepidation. Although they knew of my salvation experience, with their chilly and apathetic dispositions, they weren't about to reveal any particular concern one way or another.

Our reunion was pleasant enough though, even casual. Afterwards I spoke to them about the Lord and handed them literature and Scriptures. But they were indifferent about it for a long time. Later, their feelings became stronger—they didn't like it!

Back home in Stratford I resumed contact with Eunice's family. Mrs. Berglund was working at Sikorsky's helicopter factory while her husband Gus was still active as a building contractor. In one area of town he had built a block of beautiful colonial-style homes. He obtained permission to name one street Eunice Parkway after their daughter.

Hildur had some encouraging news for me. She had learned of a Jewish believing family who had recently moved into the area from Detroit. Isadore and Ruth Margolis were an energetic couple with two young children. Ruth had a

firm conviction about the importance of advertising. So
when they arrived in Stratford, where Isadore had a contract
to work at Sikorsky's as an aeronautical engineer, Ruth
placed a notice in the classified column of the local
newspaper: **"Seeking other Jewish believers in Jesus: Are there
any other Jewish believers in the area? If so, please contact
Margolis."**

It was like someone knocking at the door of a big open
house and calling out into the dark hallway, "Is anyone
home?" Of all the unlikely people to hear the call, it was my
brother Bunny. He noticed the quaint appeal and called it to
Hildur's attention when she came to shop in the store. (I
was still in Pennsylvania at the time.) Hildur went to visit the
Margolises.

The Margolis home was open for informal weekly
fellowship on Friday evenings. Hildur dropped in from time
to time to offer encouragement. And when I returned to
Connecticut a few months later, an introduction was
arranged at once.

We got on well from the first, and our little group began to
grow. Then Ruth was stricken with polio. Hospitalized, she
returned paralyzed from the waist down. Although confined
to her bed much of the time, she also learned to move about
in a wheelchair. The Margolis home continued to serve as a
center and eventually developed into the headquarters of a
worldwide mailing service. Literature and Scriptures were
offered free. Ruth's penchant for advertising was exploited to
the full.

Through one of the visitors at the Margolis home, I learned
about a young adult group that met every Saturday night at
Black Rock, an independent evangelical congregation in
Bridgeport. The "Saturday Nighters" combined social and

spiritual activities, and it all continued for some two decades.

I also began to attend local fellowships and to mingle with the general believing community in the area. Alma Fredericks, a quiet and faithful friend living in our neighborhood, tried to persuade me to join the independent evangelical fellowship. "Stop being a church tramp," she chided me one day. I liked the people at Black Rock. But I couldn't sense any leading to join an organized church. As I had gotten to know more and more believers and their fellowships, I found a lot to my liking in most of them, and I made many friends. In a way, it was a bit like being courted by a number of excellent suitors. One feels reluctant to hurt any of them by selecting just one as the final choice.

On a social level, unlike most of my Gentile friends, I'd never had the kind of upbringing which would make me inclined to choose a formal church affiliation. If anything, my background made me quite disinclined to such a connection.

One thing I did know: I belonged to the people of God; I was twice-born in the Messiah.

A few years passed. I was again working in the family store mornings, as well as cooking and keeping house for my three brothers. By this time, they were all thoroughly confirmed bachelors. It was the old routine. The atmosphere at home was heavy and inhospitable. We had such different views of life. I was beginning to feel that my options were becoming fewer and fewer.

I thought of going to Israel. I learned of a program set up to enable people to study modern Hebrew in a kibbutz settlement. One worked half a day and studied the other half. It sounded appealing, and I made serious inquiry about the trip. But the thought of going abroad by myself proved too hard to manage. And the Lord had other plans for me. In the end, I decided to leap back to Florida and take a course of Bible studies at the Miami Bible Institute. There I resumed contact with the Jewish fellowship in Miami Beach. It was now headed by "Pappy" Hoolsema, a jovial and fatherly pastor from Michigan. They were a very congenial mixed group of Jewish and Gentile believers, and I fit in well. At the time, the fellowship was using the auditorium of the Institute for their services and meetings.

At the Institute I also met Nancy, who became my roommate. She had come out of a troubled home in New York state. We became good friends, and at the end of the semester we decided to look for rooms and jobs in the Miami area together. We were both reluctant to return to our homes, but nothing suitable turned up. Sadly, we decided that we had to return home after all.

We booked an inexpensive flight to New York. Our hearts were heavy at the prospect of returning home. "Just forget about everything and go to sleep," the stewardess counseled us cheerfully, as she made us comfortable with pillows and blankets. We were flying above the clouds, the moon full and radiant in the dark night sky. I wondered what lay ahead. "Is it back to the old routine," I prayed silently, "the same wearisome tensions and drudgery? Surely, God, there can be another turning point in my life."

I had been wandering in the wilderness somewhat like my forefathers under Moses, moving on and yet ever circling the same mountain. *"You have compassed this mountain long enough. Turn northward ..."* (Deuteronomy 2:3) the command had once been given.

And then I was asleep. In a moment, as it seemed, I was back in the north, on my way to the family house after an eight-month sojourn in Florida.

Chapter Four

CORRESPONDENCE COURSE

The telephone rang. It was Ruth Margolis for one of our frequent heart-to-heart chats.

"Oh, Ruth," I sighed wistfully. "We've been praying so long for a partner for me! I'm so lonesome!"

"You know what?" she countered. "I've been receiving letters from a Jewish believer in New York. Don't get excited. I don't know how old he is, or what his marital status is or anything much about him. But would you be interested in corresponding with him?"

"Yes," I replied, with no little relish at the thought of—perhaps—an eligible bachelor. "What's his name and address?"

"Well, let me give him your name and address, and I'll ask him if he'd like to correspond with you. How's that?" Ruth parried.

Mr. X was notified of my existence and indicated an interest in starting a correspondence. Before he could get a letter off to me, however, I had wangled his address from Ruth, and the correspondence was on.

Mr. X—Menahem, as it turned out—had grown up in Brooklyn but was now living in Beacon, a small town in upstate New York. Our letters kept winging back and forth for a few months between New York and Connecticut. We had quickly disposed of the "pawns" in the game: Both of us were unmarried and not averse to forsaking the state of single blessedness. We were in the same age bracket. And each of us was the youngest of seven children in Jewish immigrant families.

I gathered that Menahem was something of an intellectual. I would get lengthy epistles, closely penciled, like someone preparing the rough draft of a manuscript. He would pour out his ideas, his feelings, and perhaps without realizing it, his literary longings, about two or three times a month. It was often way over my head.

"Why does he use a pencil when he writes you?" my brother Charly asked me rather sarcastically when he saw some of the letters. "Can't he afford a pen?"

Menahem was already a batter with two strikes against him when my brothers learned that he was also a Jewish believer in Yeshua. He had been born on the Lower East Side of New York City, the well-known "ghetto" into which masses of immigrant Jews had crowded during the first decades of the twentieth century. By the time he was five, the family's economic status had improved sufficiently for them to be able to move to Brooklyn.

Like most of the children of Old World parents, Menahem was quickly swept into confrontation with modern American life. Growing up during the hectic days of the Great Depression, the family abandoned many of the old separatist Jewish ways, although his parents clung to the ultra-Orthodox traditions as long as they lived.

I remember Menahem telling me how one of his sister's girlfriends visited their Brooklyn flat. She was quite talkative and not too tactful. His brother Sam asked her to what synagogue her family belonged. "Oh, we're Reformed. We think all that Orthodox way is just old-fashioned," Bessie blurted out. Menahem's father was sitting at the table, his head covered with the traditional Orthodox skullcap. He smiled wearily and sadly repeated:

"Old-fashioned, huh. Old-fashioned!"

Menahem's brother Sam tried to help save the situation with a joke, and chided Bessie. "Oh, tell him you were talking about a whiskey!"

Following the attack on Pearl Harbor, two of Menahem's older brothers entered the service. Menahem was just out of high school then, but a little over a year later, when the age level was lowered for induction, he became a U.S. Army medic. He had looked forward to military service. It was the first time he had ever been away from home, except for brief summer camp.

A popular song of that era was "The Army's Made a Man Out of Me." Like many young men of his age, Menahem was convinced that military service would be a powerful, body-building, and character-building experience. It would also solve the many problems he faced as the child of a not-too-well-adjusted immigrant family. Of course, he believed in the war wholeheartedly and the U.S. and Allies' response to Japanese militarism and Nazi-Fascist brutality.

Looking back on the experience of three years in service, even though he had no regrets, he realized it had not met his expectations. Later, he credited the army with freeing him from the control of his childhood environment, so that he could face the spiritual dilemmas of his life. While in England on duty he decided to read the New Testament seriously. But let him tell the story, as he later described it in a testimonial article he wrote.

"While I was serving in England, the novel *The Nazarene* by Sholem Asch, a prominent Yiddish writer of the early twentieth century, came to my mind again. I thought that a man like Sholem Asch, reared in traditional Judaism, emancipated, a Socialist, identified with his people, yet a man of the world, could help me to understand this strange Jew of Nazareth who loomed so large in the history of mankind. So it was that in 1944 I went rather furtively into a small town near my army base to buy my first complete Bible. I had decided that I would first have to study the source of *The Nazarene* before I could evaluate the novel based on it.

"I remember the joy I felt at reading the Sermon on the Mount and the parables. How thrilled I was at the teachings of the great Rabbi of Galilee, my kinsman according to the flesh (Romans 9:3). I committed large passages of the New Testament to memory.

"I became convinced that if there was any basis for a Jewish Messianic hope, it could only have been fulfilled in our own Rabbi Yeshua, from whom *"we hid, as it were, our faces . . . and we esteemed him not"* (Isaiah 53:3).

"I knew that accepting him and acknowledging him openly would not make me any less a Jew inwardly. It would rather be a completing of my Judaism, *"a circumcision not made with hands"* (Colossians 2:11). Yet it was extremely difficult for me, deeply rooted in Jewish life and culture, to take such a dramatic step. In the eyes of most Jews, such a commitment represents a severance from the life of Judaism and the Jewish people."

It took Menahem fourteen years of spiritual struggle to come to the point where he would openly and publicly confess his faith in Yeshua as Messiah and Redeemer.

When we had started to correspond, he was just beginning to venture into full fellowship with other believers. He was especially seeking out people of similar background. So when he saw a postcard notice from a Jewish believing fellowship in Stratford in the office of Rachmiel Frydland, a believing Jewish friend, he started to correspond with the Margolises who had sent it.

Thanksgiving was approaching, and I thought it would be an excellent idea to have Menahem over for the holiday in our quiet New England town. But he thought it was rushing things too much. Anyway, a kind Gentile family had already invited him for the holiday dinner in Beacon.

So I put in a bid for Christmas, a weekend holiday that year.

Menahem felt the hot breath of courtship—someone pursuing a bit too close for comfort. What did my friend Ruth always say, "A man chases a woman until she catches him"?

Well, I guess he didn't mind too much. He made a compromise suggestion. "We'll skip Christmas, but the New Year's weekend would be fine."

A friend of my family undertook to provide accommodations for him over the weekend. And I waited with no little anticipation for our first date.

New Year's Eve began with a gray, chilly downpour. The area was being lashed by strong winds, and a snowstorm was threatening. Menahem had to take two trains to get to our town. He decided not to wear anything especially impressive, so he said. (To tell the truth, I don't think he had any clothes that were especially impressive, although he always insisted that he did.)

When he knocked on my friend Marge's door, he really looked pathetic. He was wearing a corduroy hat, half-squashed and soaked. His umbrella had been demolished by the heavy winds and his not-very-impressive suit was drenched. For a finishing touch, his winter long johns were

sticking out from under his trousers, dripping onto the floor.
Marge looked out at her unconventional guest a bit surprised,
but kept a nonchalant expression on her face. She let him
in, helped him dry off and seated him on the sofa in the
sitting room.

My brothers and I were due in an hour for the New Year's
Eve dinner. I could hardly wait. I phoned Marge to get her
impression.

"Has he come yet?" I asked, with my characteristic
nervous giggle.

"Ye-e-s," Marge replied cautiously.

"Is he presentable, Marge?"

"Of course, yes," Marge reassured me.

An hour later, my three brothers and I marched into the
sitting room where Menahem was relaxing. I smiled coyly at
him and wiggled the fingers of my right hand "cutely" (so he
later said) at him as he stood to greet us.

"Hi," I said, followed by a toothsome smile, not a little
anxious about my brothers' reaction to him. He looked so
gaunt, so pale and so ill-clad. I suppose he aroused the
maternal instinct in me. "Poor boy, he sure needs a wife!"

But he was quite self-possessed. With a broad smile, he
greeted me and accepted a very limp and unenthusiastic
handshake from one or two of the boys.

After we had taken our coats off, Marge served a drink
and then called us all to join the family in the well-furnished
dining room, the table spread out with all the holiday
trimmings.

Trying to be sarcastic, my brother Charly asked Menahem,
"Aren't you going to say grace?" Marge and her family were
not particularly evangelical, so Menahem smiled and replied
casually, "Oh, we'll do it silently."

A few minutes later, Charly continued his line of attack, "Tell me, why do you write your letters in pencil? Don't you own a pen?"

Menahem smiled again, and responded pleasantly. "Well, with a pencil I can erase if I want to change something." "Oh," Charly grunted solemnly and continued eating. The other boys looked on expressionless and decided that further conversation was unnecessary.

Menahem and I chatted together for most of the meal, the boys talking amongst themselves and with our hosts. After dinner, I told Menahem about a New Year's Eve Watch Night service being held nearby. He agreed that we should attend. We made suitable farewells to my apathetic brothers and went out into the chilly night. We walked along the nearly empty streets to the building, a sharp wind blowing the sleet into our faces.

We mingled freely with the people in the fellowship. Before the service, a lively young people's group conducted a drama, followed by an open symposium on ethics and biblical living. I was pleased and rather proud, as Menahem threw himself into the event among people he had only just met.

"Isadore Margolis will pick us up tomorrow and we can visit with them," I told Menahem as he escorted me home around midnight and then returned to the home of our family friends with whom he was to stay.

The next day, at the Margolis home, Menahem was as articulate as ever. In fact, his informality appealed to me. He didn't seem to be nervous or ill at ease meeting new people. He must have sensed that all of us were sizing him up and that not too far back in our minds we were asking, "Is he the right one?"

I suppose you might say he was "candidating"—like ministers being called to give a trial sermon before a new congregation. Only he didn't care one whit about polishing up ahead of time. Oh, those clothes of his . . . !

Ruth consoled me. "I've heard of fellows who dress like that but have plenty stacked away under the mattress!" Ruth was usually clever and practical in such matters. But in this case, forget "stacked away." There wasn't any mattress!

Actually, Menahem was a hippie before there were hippies. To him, clothes served only two functions—to keep you warm when necessary, and to keep you decent enough to comply with the law and the minimum of social conventions. Anything else—like style, fit or current fashion—was totally irrelevant. Please don't bother him! *"Consider the lilies of the field . . . Solomon in all his glory was not arrayed like one of these"* (Matthew 6:28-29). That was one of his favorite quotations.

He was some lily, but I liked him anyway!

After the New Year's weekend, we continued a lively correspondence. The boys had been reticent about him during his first visit. But now they began to express a hostile attitude, intensified when they learned he had no financial status whatsoever. He was working in a factory, living in a cheap furnished room and a Jewish believer to boot. Charly dubbed him the *kabtzan* (the pauper), not that Menahem was asking for help or for a shoulder to cry on.

I felt more and more alienated from my brothers. I dreamed of going back to Florida—but with someone. I guess our family has the eloping spirit deeply ingrained. I wrote Menahem a passionate letter, suggesting that we elope and move to Florida. Menahem was quite surprised by the letter. He didn't like my pushiness. After a week passed without an answer, I got nervous and phoned him at the rooming house where he was boarding.

"Did you get my letter?" I asked coyly.

"Yeah," was his curt reply.

I used all my Eve-ish wiles to pacify him, but he maintained a cool masculine front. He wasn't going to be robbed of the privilege of being the pacesetter.

"Couldn't we talk about it someplace?" I suggested. He hesitated. "Well, I can't make it out to Connecticut," he replied, "but if you want to meet me halfway in Grand Central Station on Saturday, we can spend a day in New York City." I agreed.

Menahem was very cordial as we walked through Central Park. The February weather was crisp and stimulating. The lake was frozen over and people were ice skating on it. After lunch, we walked around the park, talking about the future. He told me that he couldn't rush into marriage. We had met only a few times. He liked me, but he wanted to be sure that we were right for one another. We couldn't live by worldly standards, have our fling and forget each other. If we were to be married, we had to live according to biblical norms, and that meant: *"What therefore God has joined together, let not man put asunder"* (Matthew 19:6).

He suggested that we continue to keep in touch by mail, pray earnestly about marriage, and exchange visits from time to time. Just before leaving the park to return to the station that night, Menahem wanted to kiss me.

I said, "No."

"Why?" he asked in astonishment. "You were ready for us to elope and go to Florida. And now you won't even let me kiss you?"

Now I felt we should leave things as they were; that's the way he said he wanted it.

We walked back to the station together and shook hands as I got ready to take the train back home.

"I'll be in touch," he assured me.

During the next few weeks, Menahem began to share with me some of his family background. Like me, he was the youngest of seven children. His parents, who were no longer alive, had been traditional Jewish immigrants from Galicia in East Europe. In comparison with other immigrants, they had been very devout, especially Menahem's mother, who continued to wear the Orthodox wig, the *sheitl*, even in America. The wig was a sign of submission to Jewish tradition and was popularly understood to be a means of discouraging adulterous liaisons from developing. In the New World it became a symbol to Americanized Jews of social backwardness.

When his parents moved to a Jewish neighborhood in Brooklyn, Menahem began to realize that the *sheitl* was quite offensive to other Jewish women of similar background who were in a hurry to become modern and Americanized. He explained it to me this way: "To be different from the mainstream of your community is like throwing down the gauntlet. Basically, people are intolerant of those who are out of step with the norms of their community. Even where there are no moral or legal issues involved, they find ways to express their disapproval—shunning those who are different, mocking them, making snide remarks."

It was very painful for Menahem as a child to hear his beloved mother referred to disdainfully as "the *sheitl*," and he himself singled out for abuse for some childish misbehavior on his part.

Menahem's father had had a very difficult childhood in the Galician village where he grew up. At the age of ten he had been sent away to learn tailoring, apprenticed to a harsh and stingy master who kept him half-starved even on the Sabbath.

Like almost all couples at the time, Menahem's parents' marriage had been arranged by a *shadchan* (matchmaker). Although American-raised, all their seven children grew up in the Yiddish-speaking milieu of their immigrant parents. Once they were old enough, they opted for almost total integration into modern American life. Menahem was fortunate that during his childhood, the mainstream Jewish community was coming to realize that the Old World ways would not keep American Jews attached to Orthodox Judaism. As a result, he and his peers received a good Jewish education, Zionist- and Hebrew-oriented, alongside a modern form of Orthodoxy, something he never regretted. In fact, he was the only one of his siblings who continued to practice Orthodoxy for some years after his *bar mitzvah.*

Actually, he never rejected Orthodoxy emotionally, as did his older brothers who had experienced it in the old style. In certain ways, it prepared him for the rejection that Messianic Jews experience if they choose to live as close as possible to the mainstream Jewish community. This kind of rejection is especially felt in Jerusalem.

Chapter Five

THE VOICE OF LOVE

The sturdy maples and oaks lining our street were stirring to the early signals of spring. Tuning up for their springtime serenade were bluebirds and robins, while chattering sparrows and woodpeckers were busy at their perennial tasks. Outside our house, pink and white roses were budding alongside the lilies of the valley near the reviving grass on the lawn. The nights were not so harsh, the winds somewhat gentler and we were gradually shedding our winter clothing.

Palm Sunday that year was blessed with the kind of weather one would expect—bright, sunny, hopeful—a touch of Jerusalem in New England. During the week a letter from Menahem arrived. A small slip slid out from among the sheets of letter paper. Writing of a more careful hand than usual covered the page. It was an original poem, based on the second chapter of the Song of Songs.

The voice of love is coming,
The voice of love is near,
Like mountain streams a-running,
Or hills astir with deer.
The voice of love is standing
Behind a lovely wall,
And gazes in with longing,
To make its eager call.

Rise up, my love, my fair one,
The lonely winter's gone.

Come away, come away to the Paschal Feast;
Let the songs of spring be thy bridal wreath,
With flowers and figs,
Sweet smells and sun,
Arise my love, my fair one.

It was a touching gift, and it had arrived just before my trip to the small country town where Menahem was living. He had arranged for me to stay at a local residence during the holiday weekend. He wanted me to get the feel of the town and the sense of living in a different community.

Well-organized communities usually expect people to fit into clearly defined categories. Although the Jewish community in Beacon wasn't about to ban Menahem for his belief in Yeshua, they couldn't understand why he occasionally visited the synagogue and kept up an interest in Jewish life. "You can't dance at two weddings at the same time," the local Rabbi remarked to him during a conversation about Yeshua.

Church people were also puzzled by his attitude. Like me, Menahem had no background that would lead him into a specific denomination. He just didn't feel competent to judge among the many groups and divisions in the church. Within walking distance from his room there was a Conservative Baptist church, a Nazarene church, a Salvation Army meeting hall, one Spanish-speaking and one English-speaking Assembly of God Church, two Methodist churches (which failed to merge even with declining memberships), African Methodist and black Baptist churches, a historic Dutch Reformed church, and a stately Presbyterian church. And the majority of the local citizens were at least nominally Roman Catholic or Episcopalian!

No, Menahem decided, he wasn't going to get lost in the

maze of denominations. He liked to be with people who
loved the Lord, but he also wanted to remain in living
contact with his own people, kinsmen according to the flesh
(Romans 9:3).

"In New Testament times," he once remarked, "it was
possible for Yeshua-believing Jews to worship in the Temple
and in the synagogues and at the same time to continue in
fellowship with other believers. Paul and the other Hebrew
apostles did this often."

Then came the long, tragic era of polarization. Jews and
Christians gazed out at one another from opposite camps, as
if they were mortal enemies separated by powerfully built
barricades. In modern America, these barricades had largely
been abandoned. Jews and Christians were generally aware
that it was possible to respect one another's differences
without feeling bitterness or hostility towards one another.

The Glass family of Beacon were the kind of Christians
who had a strong appreciation for God's purpose with the
Jewish people. They were a great encouragement to
Menahem. He had met Frances Glass during a visit to the
local Salvation Army meeting hall. The young officer leading
the service had asked for personal testimonies. So Menahem
got up and told of how he had come to accept Yeshua out of
a Jewish background.

After his talk, Mrs. Glass introduced herself, expressing
pleasure at meeting a Jewish believer. She spoke of her great
sympathy for the Jewish people, and of their sufferings at the
hands of Gentile churches. Menahem was invited to meet
the family during the approaching Thanksgiving feast.

It was a warm, friendly gathering, with Wesley and
Frances, their children and grandchildren. Three of them
were in full-time Christian work. Menahem remained in

regular contact with them. The following year, when they learned of my prospective visit to Beacon, they invited us both for a holiday dinner. We got on famously.

Menahem also took me around to meet the many folks he had come to know during his year in town. We also visited the local synagogue for the Sabbath service. Some of the worshippers were buzzing among themselves about my presence, wondering whether or not I was Jewish.

"Why don't you come and live in Beacon?" Menahem asked me. "We could get to know each other better. Then we could be sure about marriage."

"No, Menahem," I told him. "I don't agree. I like Beacon, but I can't come here now. Besides, what would I do here?"

"Well, we'll keep in touch," he told me, as he escorted me to the railroad station before going off to work on Monday.

Two months passed, and Menahem wrote me that there had been a general layoff at the factory. Since the mountain (me) wouldn't come to Mohammed (him), he decided to travel to the "mountain" in Stratford, Connecticut.

He phoned me to arrange another meeting in New York over the Memorial Day weekend. I could meet his family at an informal gathering in his brother Lou's apartment in Far Rockaway and stay overnight with believing friends in Manhattan.

The family received me very warmly. Although they had come from a much more traditional background than mine, they seemed to have no hangups about my belief in Yeshua. In fact, they seemed to accept me completely as a person.

On one occasion, his *Tante* (Aunt) Esther, a very traditional "Old Country" Jewish woman, asked him if I was Jewish. "Yes," he replied, "but she also believes in "Yesus" like me." She thought for a moment and then responded in

Yiddish: "As long as she's Jewish! Bring her over for dinner."

After dinner at his brother Lou's house, I sat down at the piano and started playing—and what I played best were simple old gospel songs. Menahem was a little nervous about that. Then his brother-in-law Nat sat down beside me and said, "I like the way you play." He even knew a few hymns, which he had played on the saxophone when he was younger!

We took a stroll along the Rockaway Beach promenade.

"I love you very much," Menahem told me. "I need a few days to wind up affairs in Beacon, and then I can move to Stratford. We have to bring our relationship to a conclusion."

Within two weeks he was settling down in Stratford. Ruth Margolis had arranged for him to stay in a private house not far from their home. For a very small sum, he was provided room and board in a lovely, newly-developed area of Stratford. We saw each other or spoke on the telephone daily.

He had saved up some money in Beacon and wanted to get things sorted out in his mind before starting work in Stratford. First of all, he decided to propose marriage to me. By this time, I knew that we truly belonged to one another, that our lives were bound up with one another's.

My brothers were not of the same mind. Without a job or status, with strange, unconventional beliefs, what was there to discuss about marriage?

When Menahem determined to announce our engagement to them, their response was devastating. Charly and Mendy just walked out of the room without a word of comment, but their faces spoke volumes. Bunny sat down nonchalantly on the big living room sofa near the door.

"Are you going to the West Coast?" he asked woodenly. (I

had previously mentioned the possibility of a work offer for Menahem and me in Los Angeles.) The hint was so broad and tactless that Menahem hardly knew how to keep the conversation going any further. It was after dinner, and I went into the kitchen to wash up the dishes. Menahem hurried in and helped me to finish.

"Come on, let's go out for a walk," he urged me.

After he had cooled down while we were walking, I again broached the idea of moving to Florida. But Menahem wasn't inclined to move again so quickly. "I've moved around enough in my life. I'd like to strike some roots, if possible," he replied.

Within a short time he found work at a small factory in Bridgeport that manufactured fluorescent ballasts. The work was diversified, and he enjoyed it. In July, the factory was due to close down for the annual two-week holiday. When Menahem heard this, he decided, "That's when we're going to get married."

We only had a short time to go. We had to find an apartment and furniture and make arrangements for the wedding. Menahem was working a heavy schedule at the factory. The July heat was particularly oppressive that summer. We dashed about, following newspaper leads and the suggestions of friends. Just one week before the vacation was due to begin, we found a small, two-room partly-furnished apartment. It was a ten-minute walk from the factory.

We hustled about, making preparations for the wedding. The Margolises offered us their home for a Sunday afternoon wedding. We started writing out announcements and giving word-of-mouth invitations. Isadore Margolis called Menahem up a few days before the wedding. He was alarmed.

"Menahem, your fiancée is getting carried away! She's invited more than sixty-five people! We can't have them and all the other guests in our little home." Being an engineer, he had made all sorts of calculations about building tensions and stress, floor capacity, and the like.

"But not everybody invited to a wedding automatically shows up," I insisted to Menahem when he spoke to me about Isadore's concern. Like Isadore, Menahem began making practical calculations, and decided to call up the proprietor of a nearby hall. Just in case the house was overcrowded, and just in case we couldn't move out onto the lawn because it might just possibly be a rainy day, and just in case an unforeseen disaster might occur, would the hall be available at short notice?

"Yes, sir," Menahem was assured, "for the price of ten dollars."

Of course, there were no disasters, no sudden summer thunderstorms, no moving out onto the lawn, and the "more than sixty-five" people I had invited didn't all show up. So we had a nice, comfortable more-than-roomful of guests for a sunny afternoon wedding.

A dozen of Menahem's relatives from New York drove up, along with some friends of the family. A group of our friends from the "Saturday nighters" were there to see us through. Marge and May, friends of my family, were there, but my brothers would not come. And there were my local friends, as well as a Jewish believing girlfriend from the Bronx who drove up. Hildur Berglund came; at my request she played the piano and sang during the simple service.

An attempt to have a traditional Jewish service was rebuffed when the rabbi learned that we were Jewish

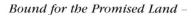

believers. As a chaplain in the U.S. Army, he knew about Messianic Jews. He was not unkind. "I can't perform the ceremony," he said. "But perhaps a Reform rabbi would."

Chapter Six

JOURNEYINGS

After our honeymoon trip to New Jersey and Pennsylvania, we returned to our new flat in Bridgeport. We discovered that we were in walking distance of several of my closest relatives. Discovered? Yes, because as close as we were by blood ties, we were quite distant in other ways.

My father had had six brothers, four of whom were living with their families in various parts of Connecticut. Yet I had had little contact with them while growing up, and almost none afterwards. Mother had been very cool to her numerous brothers-in-law and had discouraged family visits. She felt that they had taken advantage of my father's generous nature, especially in regard to supporting their aged parents. My father had been made to bear the burden at the expense of his own family.

In any case, Menahem and I decided that we should overlook family differences and re-establish a friendly relationship, since quite a few of my cousins were more or less our neighbors. I suppose word about us got around quickly. They didn't seem too shocked to learn about our beliefs.

Their general opinion was, "America's a free country. You can believe what you want, as long as it makes you happy." Their attitude was typical of comfortable, middle-class American Jewry. For many American Jews, as for their Gentile neighbors, religion is a private, pious sentiment to be indulged in very sparingly.

I think our relatives may have felt we were going too far when we decided to go house to house, offering copies of the special "Prophecy Edition" of the New Testament published by the Million Testaments Campaign. These were pocket-sized books with boldface type for the numerous New Testament passages that relate directly to the Tanakh (the "Old Testament"). This edition also contains explanatory material and cross-reference schemes designed to help Jewish people prayerfully consider the Jewishness of the New Testament writings.

We would go out in the early evening, shortly after supper, and ring the doorbells of the homes in the neighborhood. If the occupants were Jewish, we would offer them the New Testament on condition they promised to read it. If they were Gentile, we would leave Gospel literature. We were almost always received politely and were sometimes invited into homes, where we would have lively discussions.

"That must refer to Jesus Christ, I suppose," remarked one earnest Jewish housewife, a part-time Hebrew teacher. We had just completed reading Isaiah 53 from a recognized Jewish translation into English. She and her husband, an electrician by trade, were convinced followers of traditional Judaism. It was more than a pious sentiment or incidental part of their lives. They testified to an abiding faith in God.

"Isn't it possible," she asked after a while, "that Jesus' life and work were for the Gentiles, while we have our *Torah*?"

No amount of reasoning from the Scriptures could persuade them that this would be incompatible with the teachings of the Bible. However, this is a view that many liberal Jews have come to accept. Before we left, they consented to join us in prayer. They bowed their heads as we prayed that the Spirit of God would persuade them that the New Testament and Yeshua were still relevant for Jews.

We had a particularly gratifying experience in one house shortly after the beginning of our circuit. We encountered a second-generation Jewish American family who were completely open to us. Joe and Mary invited us again and again to come and visit with them. We met their two daughters and their son-in-law, all of whom expressed a warm interest in the gospel. We would go together to meetings at the Margolises and also visit many evangelical congregations in the area. Joe, after making a clear profession of faith, pressed forward spontaneously to fulfill the ordinance of full immersion.

After a while, my brothers became reconciled to us. They even came over for dinner one evening. I cooked them a full-course, old-fashioned Jewish meal. Charly couldn't resist a sarcastic dig along with the pleasantries. Looking over our very—shall I say—snug apartment, he commented, "Well, it's a good thing we don't have claustrophobia, or this could be very hard to take." But by the end of the evening, Charly, who had a very fine singing voice, was actually joining in with Menahem and me as we sang gospel songs and a musical setting that Menahem had composed for his poem "The Voice of Love." I merrily squeezed away at my twelve-bass Italian-made accordion. We were invited to come over to the cottage the following spring, and Bunny graciously showed Menahem around.

All in all, we spent a year in Connecticut. Then, in striking response to prayers for guidance offered by believing friends, we were impressed that we should move down to Miami Beach, Florida. This was the very place of my salvation and my first experience of fellowship in Yeshua.

Menahem served notice at the factory. "We hate to see you go," said the boss. Menahem had had many occasions to speak about the Lord to him and the workers. Most were Protestant or Catholic churchgoers who couldn't quite understand a Jewish believer in Yeshua. But they appreciated his diligence and faithfulness at work.

Our many friends and acquaintances in the Jewish and Christian communities were very kind to us. We left Connecticut feeling we had been the recipients of much blessing from the Lord and His people, and we looked forward with anticipation to life in Florida.

When we arrived in Miami, my sister's husband Eli and their younger daughter Glenna picked us up and took us home with them. It was a pleasant reunion, and they seemed to like Menahem. They invited us to stay for a few weeks. But we saw that they were quite cramped, and after a few days we looked around Miami Beach and found a neat little "pulmanette." It was a large room with a kitchen alcove and bathroom adjoining, at a bargain rate during the summer off season. We were only two blocks from the seashore, and Menahem was quite entranced by the exotic beauty of the area. It was his first trip to Florida.

It was good to renew fellowship with the congregation on the beach. The well-beloved Pastor A.J. Hoolsema was assisted by several younger men and women. The congregation had grown considerably, with regular meetings for worship and gospel preaching. There was a steady witness to tourists, residents, young people and especially to the large, permanent Jewish community, which earned Miami Beach the nickname of "Little Israel."

We were offered employment with the congregation as

staff members. Menahem, however, felt that it would be better to do regular work and help in the fellowship and witness as lay members of the congregation. After a very discouraging period of job hunting (including a depressing attempt to become a printing salesman), he took work at the Dade County Jackson Memorial Hospital in Miami as a surgical orderly. Menahem had been introduced to medical work while in the U.S. Army. It was work that he found most satisfying, and he had held several similar jobs in civilian medical institutions after leaving the army.

We were soon deeply involved in the congregational fellowship and in the life of the community. Menahem found the work at the hospital very rewarding, first in the operating room theater and then as an aide in the surgical recovery room.

Meanwhile, we started searching for a permanent place to live. We certainly couldn't afford to stay in the pulmanette. When the winter season began, the hotel keeper would demand literally ten times the weekly rental we were paying, although that would include communal meals.

Believers were very active in the area, but Jewish residents were often resistant. Though far from fanatical, many were quite traditional. You might say there was a spirited dialogue between them and us.

There was one vigorous evangelist, Charles Cline, who had an open air ministry at the crowded Lincoln Mall and on Miami Beach, whom we visited from time to time. There were always knots of people, especially Jewish people, who gathered round as he offered Bibles and literature, and very determinedly exhorted passersby. He preached a very unsophisticated message, which often enraged his younger hearers, both Jewish and Gentile.

One Sunday afternoon at the beach, Charly Cline and
Menahem were speaking before a group of bathers when an
adjacent cafe owner decided that it wasn't good for his
business. Every time Menahem or Charly started to talk, the
proprietor turned on his loudspeaker, blaring the most raucous
music you could imagine. At first, Menahem and Charly tried to
talk above the blare, but then they had to stop—and the music
stopped. They started talking again, and the music began again.
It was something like the wheels in Ezekiel's vision. This went
on for some ten minutes. I forget who won, but it generated
plenty of attention and certainly didn't put an end to the
witness on the beach.

I began to look for work in the area, but found only
temporary jobs. The fellowship offered me a part-time job.
Menahem was quite happy at his hospital work. He would
start off for the hospital at 5:20 A.M. and return home late in
the afternoon. Then he was off to the seashore for his daily
dip. We would have prayer and Bible reading, go out to visit
friends, take part in congregational activities and continue our
search for more permanent living quarters. We were content,
and looking forward to a settled life in southern Florida.

Our first anniversary came, and Menahem produced a
sequel to "The Voice of Love." This was a four stanza mosaic
of Scripture, mainly from the Song of Songs, which he
entitled "My Lovely Garden: A First Anniversary Ode
(7/30/1962)."

I am come into my garden
O my sister, o my spouse!

See how many gifts are mine!
Spice and honey
Milk and wine.

flocks of sheep
And eyes of doves
A thousand shields
And fairest loves!

I am come into my garden
Beside an olden house
Where we shall feed till shadows flee away.

One day, we were having our daily Bible reading. We had been reading through the book of Numbers. It was September 20, and the portion we were reading was Chapter 10. We came to verses 11-13: *"In the second year, in the second month, on the twentieth day of the month, the cloud was taken up from over the tabernacle of the testimony, and the people of Israel set out by stages from the wilderness of Sinai; and the cloud settled down in the wilderness of Paran. They set out for the first time at the command of the Lord by Moses."*

It occurred to us that that very day was the twentieth day of the second month in the second year of our life together. We were somehow moved by the coincidence. Or was it merely a coincidence? Beyond the coincidence, was the Lord telling us to move on?

Menahem had long felt the force of the Lord's admonition, *"Let your loins be girded and your lamps burning"* (Luke 12:35). This was a clear reference to Moses' command to the Israelites at the first Passover: *"In this manner you shall eat it: your loins girded, your sandals on your feet, and your staff in your hand"* (Exodus 12:11). He had made many moves of faith in the spirit of those words as the Lord spoke to his heart. And had we not come down to Miami by faith? Perhaps we were facing another command to move along in the wilderness journey of our pilgrimage. As the author of the epistle to the Hebrews had observed: *"For here we have no lasting city, but we seek the city which is to come"* (Hebrews 13:14).

Menahem debated with himself and with me. After a difficult period of readjustment, we were beginning to feel at home here: stimulating work, new friends, renewed fellowship, active witness—and not least, the relaxing and healthful surroundings of surf and sea only minutes from our door.

"Where to now, O Lord?"

Chapter Seven

THE FLEECE OF WOOL

"Come and join us in Israel. You'll find work and fellowship with other believers here." This was the tenor of several letters we had been receiving from a leader among the Jewish believers. Rachmiel Frydland was a child of the East European Polish ghetto. He had accepted the Messiah as a young man after he had abandoned traditional rabbinical studies in disgust over the rigid, hidebound methods employed in East Europe. This was a short time before the outbreak of the Second World War. By a series of miracles, he survived the dreadful Holocaust which took the lives of six million Jews, including his entire family and first wife.

After the war, Rachmiel went to England, where he studied at a Bible College. Following graduation, he accepted a post on the Lower East Side of New York as director of Hermon House, an evangelical witness to the Jewish people.

One day, he announced that he believed unattached Jewish believers should respond to the challenge of the modern movement of return to Zion. At the time, he was still unmarried, as was Menahem, and he invited Menahem to join him. Rachmiel was offered and accepted the post of Israel Secretary of the International Messianic Jewish Alliance in Haifa. After two months in Israel, he married Estelle, a soft-spoken, demure Jewish believer who had emigrated from France. Then he started pressing us to join the small band of believers in Israel.

Like me, Menahem felt inadequate to meet the challenge

of Israel. At that time, it was exceptional to hear of even mainstream American Jews going to settle in Israel. And we were outspoken believers in Yeshua!

"Many of our people," my husband wrote later, "were convinced that their greatest enemies were believers in Yeshua. To their way of thinking, the Nazis were Christians, as were all others (in the Middle East or the West) who were not Jewish or Muslim. We would seem like traitors who had joined the camp of a vicious enemy."

Were we really strong enough, rooted in our faith and in our commitment as Jews and followers of Yeshua, to withstand these pressures? These were some of the thoughts on our hearts and lips as we considered, in the days following, the possibility that the Lord might be leading us out again, this time to the homeland of our fathers.

Finally, my husband prayed a "Gideon prayer," after the pattern of Judges 6:36, *"Behold, I am laying a fleece of wool on the threshing floor; if there is dew on the fleece alone, and it is dry on all the ground, then I shall know."* I remember him lying on the bed, musing half aloud and half to himself—"Lord, grant us a sign of your leading, someone who knows nothing of our thoughts in this matter. Let him be led to send us a gift of money within a month, advising us to move to Israel. This would serve as a token of your leading." And we dismissed it from our thoughts, relaxing into our busy pattern of living.

It was indeed a strange prayer. We had spoken to absolutely no one about our thoughts, and written to no one. We had never given Rachmiel any encouragement that we were thinking of yielding to his persuasion.

Almost a month later, when we had all but forgotten the matter, we unexpectedly received a cash gift in the mail from my husband's brother-in-law, Don. Only three months earlier, he had sent us a handsome gift for our first wedding anniversary. So we were all the more impressed when he wrote that he felt that we might be needing the money. In the course of the letter, he commented about the plight of the Jews in Nazi Germany and how foolish many were who had not fled while there was still time to escape. He was comparing it to the 1962 crisis over Soviet missiles in Cuba; he saw it as a kind of parallel crisis—a "handwriting on the wall" for America.

Well, there was no direct urging for us to go to Israel—but were we tempting God? We bowed before the Lord, as we realized how inadequate we were to make what seemed then like a very drastic decision to emigrate from the U.S.

We remembered that in Gideon's case, he had put out the fleece twice—*"Please, let me make a test once more with the fleece, let it now be dry only on the fleece, and let there be dew on all the ground." And God did so* (Judges 6:39-40). So we prayed, "Lord, we'll make inquiries and plans for a possible move, letting friends know something of our thoughts, and ask for their prayers—and nothing more. If by the end of November we receive another unsolicited gift, we will accept it as a definite sign that we are to make our personal return to Zion."

So we went ahead with inquiries concerning bookings for passage to Israel, obtaining information about settling, and asking our friends to pray with us.

It was the day before Thanksgiving, the last week in November. My husband returned from duty at the hospital, anticipating a restful weekend at home. I set before him the airmail letter we had received that same day from Rachmiel Frydland in Haifa.

"I am sending you, without your request, the enclosed check for $15.00, which is the only American money I have at hand. I want you to make preparations to come to Israel."

My husband smiled upon reading it, threw the letter down, and exclaimed, "Well, I guess it's settled—we go!"

That same afternoon, we went down to an Israeli shipping office in Miami to begin the arrangements for booking passage.

Chapter Eight

FROM THE ENDS OF THE EARTH

We booked passage on an Israeli freighter, the M/V Beersheva. Because of a prolonged U.S. stevedore strike, the entire schedule had been changed, but finally the strike was settled, and we were notified that the ship would arrive shortly in Miami Harbor for a one-day layover. The vessel was a beautiful cargo carrier, only two years in service. We had a cabin and shower adjoining the captain's quarters. On February 7, 1963, we boarded the ship.

My sister Sally came down to see us off, along with many of our friends from the Miami area. Because of the rearranged schedule, the ship turned west, steaming along the shores of the Gulf of Mexico, loading and discharging cargo. We stopped at Tampa, Panama City, Mobile, New Orleans, Houston. As we kept moving westward day after day Menahem wrote wistfully to Rachmiel in Haifa, "My heart is in the East, but we keep moving to the ends of the West."

Finally, the ship completed its run of the Gulf ports and turned east. On February 28, we reached North Carolina and loaded the final cargo on deck. We turned eastward for Haifa. The following eighteen days were heavy, nonstop travel, much of it through stormy Atlantic seas, until we reached our final destination.

The trip itself provided a good introduction to Israel. The Jewish officers and crew were a living portrait of biblical prophecies being fulfilled. We read Isaiah's words, *"I will*

*bring your offspring from the east, and from the west I
will gather you; I will say to the north, Give up, and to the
south, Do not withhold; bring my sons from afar and my
daughters from the end of the earth"* (Isaiah 43:5-6).

We heard many personal accounts from the lips of crew
members detailing their response to the call of Zion. There
was an Iraqi Jewish youth who had studied Hebrew and
Zionist lore in a clandestine group in Baghdad. Discovered by
the police, he had had to flee with his comrades to Iran, and
had then been flown on to Israel. There was a young
Afghanistani Jew whose family had joined a band of Jews
entering Palestine during the days of the British mandate.
There was Mischa, a burly and brash Russian Jew. He had
joined the Red Army after his father was murdered by the
Nazis during the German invasion of Russia. Later, he met up
with soldiers of the Jewish Brigade in postwar Europe. With
their aid, he slipped into Palestine past the British blockade
established to bar Jewish "illegal" immigrants clamoring to
enter the Land.

There were the familiar tales of Jews from Central Europe
surviving the Nazi terror, or fleeing just ahead of it. There
were Middle Eastern Jews who had fled the rising tide of
Arab nationalism and the anti-Jewish ferment which often
accompanied it. Others, like the handsome, dark-skinned
Yemenite Jews, were sure the return was messianic. When
they were taken in airplanes—which many saw for the first
time in their lives—in order to make the trip to the Holy
Land, they were convinced that God's word to Moses was
being fulfilled, *"I bore you on eagles' wings and brought
you to myself"* (Exodus 19:4).

Among the crew were descendants of Spanish Jews who
had been banished from Spain by the fanatical Inquisition
and the Jewish expulsion of 1492, and had settled in the

Balkans. There were Jews from many lands who had come in their youth under the impetus of the Zionist vision, and also sons of the early pioneers born in the Land. We met an American Jewish seaman working his way across to see the Land, hoping to call it home. In New Orleans, we met two Israelis on a sister ship who had come from Bombay in India and Shanghai in China.

There was also a sprinkling of non-Jewish personnel on board—from the Iberian peninsula, from the Netherlands and from Greece. Modern Jewish seamen were still a recent development; the proverbial wandering Jews had been reluctant to make the sea a permanent career.

We sensed the ironies of history among the ship's complement. The Jewish Master of the vessel had been evacuated from Austria in his childhood in the wake of German Nazi terror. Now he was commanding a ship that had been built by the German government and given to Israel without cost as part of the reparations agreement for the crimes committed by the Third Reich against the Jewish people.

One incident stands out for its striking picture of history in capsule. The third mate, a young Spanish Gentile, caught sight of a passing ship one night while we were on deck. Maritime courtesy calls for an exchange of signals by means of blinker lights. For several minutes, signals were exchanged between the two ships. Suddenly the light of the passing ship abruptly darkened. The mate roared with laughter, and cried out with contempt. "Silencio!"

"What's happened?" we asked. "It was a ship from Saudi Arabia," he replied. "As soon as I signalled our home port as Haifa, they stopped dead, and ignored all further signals from me. What foolishness—and how they hate Israel!"

Had the Arabs known the historical picture represented by a Spanish mate on a vessel built by Germans for a Jewish State, would it have taught them something of the futility of hatred for Israel? Today, we see the great power of Satan in the world, but someday he will not have this power. We can see how nations and systems based on hatred of Jews time and again have been severely judged by God: ancient Babylon, medieval Spain, Czarist Russia, Nazi Germany. Do people ever learn from history?

The Jewish seamen and officers on the M/V Beersheva were congenial as we shared our faith in Yeshua. It was no surprise. Book distributors regularly passed out Bibles in various languages at ports of call without interference.

On March 10 we passed through Gibraltar. It was also Purim, the Feast of Esther, and a costume party was organized during the evening. The wife of the "donkeyman" designed some costumes for Menahem and me. I was dressed as a cowgirl, Menahem as a Beduin. The poor chap who won the prize for the best costume had smeared himself from head to foot with oil grease, covered himself with burlap bags, and appeared as a black minstrel.

We steamed along the Mediterranean for several days, enjoying the warm sunlight and the pleasant patches of Mediterranean coastline. Then came the announcement: "We shall be in Haifa on Sunday morning, March 17." We radioed the Frydlands in Haifa about our expected arrival and prepared for disembarkation.

It was a foggy and chilly March morning as we went up on deck to catch our first glimpse of Israel early Sunday morning. The Bay of Haifa was crowded with passenger and merchant ships. We peered out expectantly at the close-packed, three-level city rising up from the seaside, spotted with sizeable patches of greenery along the slopes of Mount Carmel.

We were quickly piloted into the Bay and anchored a few hundred yards from the shore. Customs officials clambered on board, followed shortly by family and friends of the crew, who came on from a launch. There was all the hubbub of a ship's arrival. We made our farewells to the captain and crew, and some of the wives who had accompanied them on the voyage.

Estelle Frydland came on board to welcome us and to take us to their home. Her husband Rachmiel had had to be in Jerusalem for the weekend. Soon we were directed to the launch and dropped onto the shore. As we stepped onto land, following an ancient Hebrew custom prescribed for those entering the Holy Land for the first time, my husband knelt and kissed the ground, uttering the ancient Hebrew blessing: "Blessed art Thou, O Lord, our God, ruler of the world, who hast sustained us, maintained us, and caused us to attain unto this season."

Two more of Zion's exiles had returned home.

When the Lord restored the captive ones of Zion, we were like those who dream (Psalm 126:1).

Chapter Nine

AT THIS TIME

The morning chill had disappeared. The afternoon was warm and relaxing. After lunch, we took our first stroll in the new land among the hilly streets and byways winding around the slopes of Mount Carmel at the Center level, the Hadar. Every sight and sound was fresh and exciting.

The children around us were chattering in Hebrew, "the tongue of the prophets." The sacred tongue, once buried in the tomes of scholars and religious tradition, was now revived as living speech.

We thought of Mount Carmel, where Elijah waged his battle against the prophets of Baal. Cars, buses, trucks whizzed about us, honking impatiently at one another and at the briskly moving pedestrians navigating the difficult ups and downs of Haifa's streets. We were fascinated by the contrasts which strike the eye in Israel. There was the old European Orthodox Jew with his skull cap, the yarmulke, the long black coat, the caftan. Past him walked the informal, open-collared, hatless young Israeli natives, neatly dressed businessmen, Arabs with traditional kafiya head-dress and sash, Jewish immigrants from India attired in their colorful saris, workers in overalls, housewives, and young women nattily dressed.

My husband pointed in surprise to a Hebrew sign over a rather rickety structure off to the side of the main street. The words were from the Hebrew Bible, Isaiah 53:5: Vehu mehulal mi-psha'aynu, *"He was wounded for our transgressions."* It excited our curiosity.

Since this is a text that points to Yeshua as the Messiah and is not given prominence in ordinary Jewish circles, we drew close to the building and learned that it was called Bethesda Hall. When we returned from our walk, Estelle told us it was a meeting place for believers in the style of the Plymouth Brethren. It was used for communion, gospel preaching and worship, and there would be a meeting that evening.

When we returned to Bethesda in the evening, we found a small group of people assembled in a dimly-lit hall. The meeting was presided over by an elderly Russian, brother Marchinkowsky. He had left his native land after the Bolshevik revolution, after serving a term of imprisonment for his faith. Joining a group of emigrés, they had formed a settlement in the Holy Land where they had raised their families and established themselves in the community. One of them had been a charter member of the Israeli Egged bus cooperative. One son had fought and died in Israel's War of Independence. They were respected by the Jewish community.

There were also Armenians and Arabs in the congregation. In fact, the meeting was conducted in several languages. This was quite typical of many Israeli assemblies. In a subsequent gathering at this hall, my husband counted seven languages in use. They were either translated consecutively from the platform or whispered simultaneously among small clusters of people scattered about the hall—Hebrew, English, German, Russian, Yiddish, Arabic and Romanian.

After the meeting, we met the Zeidan family and went home with them for supper further up the mountainside. Mrs. Freda Zeidan had come to Israel from Nazi Germany shortly before the outbreak of World War II. She came from a family of well-known Jewish believers, the Buksbazens. Her parents remained in Germany and were eventually destroyed in the Nazi death camps, along with countless other Jews.

Freda met and married Salim Zeidan, an Arab Christian. They had begun raising a family of two boys and two girls when Salim took sick and died. Through the crises of post-war Palestine and the bitter dilemmas of the Arab-Jewish wars, she succeeded in rearing her family faithful to the Lord and devoted to all of Israel's people.

Later that evening, we had a visit from Richard Stoehr, whom Menahem had known from the U.S. He was an Austrian Jewish refugee who had settled in Sweden and later married an American woman from a family of Jewish believers, the Gitlins, and then decided to settle in Jerusalem. When he learned of our arrival, he came over to welcome us. He told us that we were the first married couple of American stock to settle in Israel as Jewish believers.

The next day, Rachmiel Frydland returned from Jerusalem. With characteristic energy, he had made all kinds of arrangements for us to meet people and obtain information about the prospects for new settlers. He was then Israel Secretary for the International Messianic Jewish Alliance. His home in Haifa was a center for believers throughout the land. In his little Volkswagen, he made periodic trips around the country, providing pastoral care for the scattered believers.

That night, a group of Jewish believers from East Europe were gathered in the Frydland home for a weekly prayer meeting and Bible study. Most of them were ordinary working people, middle aged and elderly, who represented some of the results of a considerable evangelism among Jewish people in East Europe before the war. They sang hymns in Romanian and Yiddish with great fervor and devotion.

My husband was asked to give the message in Yiddish. He spoke of the significance of Ezekiel's vision of the dry bones: "And as I looked, there were sinews on them, and flesh had come upon them, and skin had covered them; but there was no breath in them" (Ezekiel 37:8). The word translated "breath" in the English Bible is "ruach," a word which also means "spirit." Menahem expounded on the work of God in creating a natural framework for Israel at this time prior to the prophesied outpouring of His Spirit upon the regathered people. Did not Paul teach that if there is a physical body, there is also a spiritual body: *"But it is not the spiritual which is first but the physical, and then the spiritual"* (1 Corinthians 15:46). The time of Israel's spiritual rebirth will come. *"My dwelling place shall be with them; and I will be their God, and they shall be my people"* (Ezekiel 37:27).

We began to visit believers in different parts of Israel. We went to Tiberias by Lake Kinneret (the New Testament's "Sea of Galilee"), where a handful of believers now lived. Here, multitudes of Galileans had once flocked to hear the words and see the signs of the marvelous Rabbi Yeshua of Nazareth.

We visited some families of new immigrants, Jewish believers from Romania, in Upper Nazareth, "a city set on a hill." It was now a Jewish settlement overlooking the ancient city where Yeshua had grown up. Old Nazareth was the largest Arab town in Israel, with a population roughly divided between Christians and Muslims.

Most Christians in Nazareth, as throughout the whole Middle East, were members of traditional churches. They had strong communal ties. Among them it was believed that one was born a Christian or a Jew or a Muslim. And one normally remained attached to the community of one's birth for life, according to this tradition. Doctrinal positions, beliefs and moral practices were all secondary to communal ties. There were Christians and Muslims who had no religious beliefs and, as among extreme secular Jews, lived in total disregard of the principles of their community's religion. Yet they would be registered and identified as Christians, Muslims or Jews by religion. They would be baptized, circumcised, married and buried according to the rites of their community's tradition.

Here and there, Christian groups had sprung up that rejected this hereditary outlook on faith. Under the impact of Western Christian missionary efforts, they had broken with the traditional churches and were organized denominationally into various Protestant groups.

Among the Muslims, the concept of community religion remained much stronger than in the Jewish community. It was virtually unheard of at the time for a Muslim to identify him or herself openly with Christians, whether by a confession of faith in Yeshua or by joining the Christian community.

We got firsthand impressions about the problems facing believers, whether Jewish or Gentile, in the land where the Christian faith was born. Out of Israel had come the revolutionary message of a faith that comes not by natural birth but by spiritual rebirth. *"Unless one is born anew, he cannot see the kingdom of God"* (John 3:3). But in Israel, the term "Christian" was now given an ethnic sense.

Just a few months prior to our arrival, there had been something of a challenge to this system. A Carmelite monk named Brother Daniel had appealed to the Supreme Court of Israel for a ruling on his petition for full citizenship under Israel's Law of Return. This law, enacted shortly after the establishment of the State, granted every Jewish immigrant the option of citizenship upon arrival in Israel.

Brother Daniel had been born into a Polish Jewish family and given the name Oswald Rufeisen. When Poland fell to the German invaders in 1939, Rufeisen, in order to survive, represented himself as a German-speaking Pole and found work as a translator for the Gestapo. At the same time, he worked as a liaison agent with the anti-German underground. He rescued many Jews and resistance fighters, but was eventually betrayed by a collaborator. He fled to a monastery for shelter, disguising himself as a monk. Some time later, he converted to Catholicism and joined the Carmelite order which had sheltered him.

After the war, he asked to be transferred to the order's main center on Mount Carmel. He then decided to apply for citizenship as a Jew of Catholic religion under Israeli law. His request was turned down all along the line, and he finally appealed to the highest court. In a majority decision, the Court rejected his petition for citizenship under the Law of Return, but did recommend that he be given citizenship as a naturalized immigrant under a citizenship law applying to non-Jews. This he was granted.

We met Brother Daniel at the Frydland home shortly following our arrival. He had been invited by a Polish Jewish believer to present his views at a monthly meeting of believers. He had a youngish, mild-mannered look to him. Speaking in a highly-cultivated, soft-spoken voice, and wearing thin-rimmed spectacles, one was tempted to take him for a typical middle-class Jewish intellectual or scholar—except for his monk's robes!

Some of the local believers admired the monk's boldness. After all, he had openly challenged the people and the State of Israel to accept Jews who believe in Yeshua on the same basis on which they accept various other Jews—Orthodox, liberal, or atheistic. But there were those who were quite dubious about the extreme form in which Brother Daniel had confronted the State. He was a celibate Roman Catholic monk from Poland, a land whose clergy and populace had often been notoriously hostile to the Jewish people and to Judaism.

"Israel is an atheistic theocracy," he told the assembled believers.

By means of this paradoxical statement, Brother Daniel sought to convey the meaning of modern Israeli life, in which both religious and irreligious elements form the governed and the government. The old principle of Jewishness being completely bound up with Jewish religious tradition was gone. Once, it had been accepted to exclude from the community all Jews who turned aside from the dominant Jewish religious tradition—whether they were simply unbelievers, heretics or followers of Yeshua. But now, Brother Daniel argued, it was inconsistent and illogical to do so.

Unlike the majority of Jewish believers, Brother Daniel regarded himself as Jewish nationally and ethnically but not by religion. The vast majority of Jewish believers do not see themselves as abandoning the Jewish religion. They stand with Paul, the great apostle to the Gentiles, who in every encounter with his people affirmed and reaffirmed his faith as Jewish. He regularly attended the synagogue both in the Land and in the Diaspora.

In Tel-Aviv, Jerusalem and Beersheva, there were also small groups of believers in Yeshua, living in the midst of their own people, sharing the hazards and hopes of Israeli life. We were becoming part of these hopes and hazards. But it was discomforting to realize that, however understandable prophetically, we Messianic Jews remained spiritually in exile. The ancient cry of those first Jewish apostles to their risen Lord still rang clear: *"Will you at this time restore the kingdom to Israel?"* (Acts 1:6)

Chapter Ten

"As Them That Dream"

Spring was in full bloom as we moved about Galilee and the north of Israel, visiting ancient shrines and modern sites. The timelessness of the land bore witness to the perennial freshness of the "Song of Songs." Mount Carmel was ablaze with floral color and abundant fragrance during the Passover season.

After the first dreamful days, we wanted to get our bearings in the country before taking a decisive step. Various proposals were put to us. In Haifa, hospital work was available. There were invitations to join in the work of missionary societies. There were openings in several Christian schools. There was a heavy demand for native English-language teachers.

One day, Molly Kagan, a German Jewish believer and a social worker living on Mount Carmel, visited Rachmiel Frydland. She was convinced that we should enter a kibbutz—a rural communal settlement—for a period of orientation to the country. She had a point: Israel could be astonishing, even exotic, to the tourist and dreamer—but quite bewildering and complex to a new settler trying to find his roots in the "old-new land."

One morning, we went down to the Jewish Agency in Haifa. The Agency was founded in order to assist new immigrants in a variety of ways. We entered the crowded ante-room, patiently waiting our turn to see an official about the possibility of finding a kibbutz for us.

Everyone in the room, except perhaps us, seemed to be in the most desperate straits. For this group of young Jews from Brazil, a flat was an urgent necessity; someone else needed a loan in order to establish a business; this couple from Italy were living with their family in a truck; that person had educational problems to be sorted out. Everyone's patience was exhausted, at an end, utterly strained. All were commencing a new life, and not a minute could be wasted.

The atmosphere was somewhat like a maternity ward with the expectant fathers and relatives impatiently pacing the floors awaiting the news. From time to time, shouts and angry voices were heard, doors were slammed, all providing the background for a scenario in bedlam.

Finally we got to see an official, an American Jewish settler. His face was drawn and taut. He looked like a man under siege. Our conversation was constantly interrupted by phone calls, by other officials barging in and out of the office, by immigrants knocking on the door and demanding immediate attention. He made some suggestions and gave us the names of some kibbutz settlements which we could visit and decide about moving.

In all, we visited more than a dozen settlements. Not everyone was willing to accept people who were not candidates for memberships or taking part in a regular program. But first, a word about this type of settlement for those who may be unfamiliar with it.

The Hebrew word *"kibbutz"* literally means "a gathering." It was during the early part of the twentieth century when the Zionist movement was gaining momentum that the first experiments in this style of communal living were made. Faced with the tremendous challenge of reclaiming waste lands in unfriendly surroundings, the common life seemed to many of the pioneer settlers a natural solution. The impact of socialist idealism, which was very strong among East European Jews at that time, was also a powerful factor behind the kibbutz movement.

Communal life is nothing new under the sun. Throughout history, there have been groups who adopted this lifestyle, which was also current in the early Jerusalem community of believers: *"And all who believed were together and had all things in common"* (Acts 2:44f, 4:32f). The Hutterites have lived the common life for centuries. In recent years, the Jesus Movement among American youth gave communal life a renewed spur.

In time, over two hundred communal settlements were established in Israel. Most are based on secular principles, but a small number, about ten, adhere to a strictly Orthodox Jewish lifestyle. The entire movement represents only about three percent of the total Israeli population. However, they have had a great impact on the agricultural, political and military life of the country. Like any well-organized, dedicated group of people, they could take on tasks far out of proportion to their small numbers. Over the years, much of the spartan zeal of the early pioneers slackened and the idealism behind the movement waned, the desire for material success waxed, and routine patterns of living became fixed.

Through the Frydlands we met a young Frenchwoman, Janine, who was living on a kibbutz in Lower Galilee. She was one of many young non-Jews who were drawn to Israel and the common life. For many Europeans, Israel was seen as a kind of "last frontier" of civilization, offering challenging adventures, ideas and experiences. These people would sign up for a half-year ulpan (language seminar), spending half a day studying modern Hebrew and half a day working within the communal setup. The work might be in the fields, in the large communal kitchen, in the children's houses or in an industrial plant if the settlement had one. Room and board and clothes were provided, together with small monthly allowances of pocket money. One hardly needed money within the settlement itself—there weeks could go by without the need to touch "filthy lucre"; but if one ventured out into the cold, cruel world outside, it could be quite useful.

Janine suggested that we apply to a nearby settlement, Kibbutz Mizra. She thought they would be interested in accepting people outside their regular program who were willing to work. We went over to make inquiries one evening during the youth festival of Lag Ba'Omer. Beautiful well-tended gardens covered the area. There were tree-lined promenades, a large ivy-covered dining hall and cultural center, and a large swimming pool. Yet it had a quiet village atmosphere, with some seven hundred men, women and children in residence at the time.

We found our way to the home of the settlement secretary. It was a small apartment, nicely furnished. Ruth, the secretary for that year, was a Jewish woman from Germany who had immigrated to British Mandatory Palestine during the Nazi persecution. An attractive, dark-haired, personable woman, she spoke excellent English and received us courteously over a cup of coffee.

When we described our purpose, Ruth informed us that it could be arranged for us to live and work in the settlement on a temporary basis. We then told her that we were Jews who believed in Yeshua as Messiah and in the New Covenant. Would that, we asked, present any obstacle?

"No," Ruth assured us. "We aren't religious ourselves, and

your beliefs are your own private affair. There's no reason why they should make you unacceptable, as long as you don't agitate or do anything to disrupt the life of the settlement."

"Obviously we won't do anything to disrupt things, since we would be your guests," my husband responded. "But what if people ask questions as we're talking? You know how these things develop. We wouldn't want to feel that we can't discuss our beliefs in the normal course of a conversation."

Ruth was quick to reassure us that they believed in freedom of speech. "We have no objection to anyone knowing what you believe, even though we ourselves are not religious," she reiterated.

We learned that the settlement was part of the small left-wing Socialist party Mapam, who regard their Jewishness as purely a national or ethnic affair. In their lifestyle, all purely religious values and symbols were either secularized or eliminated. Thus the Sabbath, that kingpin of Jewish Orthodoxy, was observed solely as a day off, like Sunday in nominally Christian countries. Biblical festivals such as Passover, Pentecost and Tabernacles, were given agricultural and folkloristic interpretations and celebrated without religious observances. As for the Day of Atonement—Yom Kippur—it was virtually ignored, except as an extra holiday. All the traditional dietary laws, synagogue rites and ceremonies were disregarded. The Hebrew Bible was studied, but only as literature, history and ancient Hebrew culture.

After our conversation, Ruth introduced us to the Oren family, who were leaders of the settlement. Mordecai Oren was also a leader in the political movement to which the kibbutz belonged. His wife Rega was in charge of Hebrew language instruction.

While the ladies chatted in Hebrew, Mordecai engaged us in conversation in English, which he spoke quite well. He seemed interested to learn more about our American Jewish background.

"With which of the Jewish religious movements were you affiliated in the States?" he asked. "Were you Orthodox, Conservative or Reform?"

"Not with any," my husband replied.

"Oh, no? Then what kind of Jewish community life did you have?" he continued.

In good Jewish fashion, my husband replied to one question with another. "Have you ever heard of Jewish believers in Yeshua?" he asked.

"Oh yes," Mordecai responded, with a smile which suggested neither surprise nor dismay. "I was a political prisoner in Czechoslovakia for a number of years. There was such a believer in prison with me during that time. Tell me, are there many such people in America?"

We discussed the movement in America briefly and then the ladies rejoined the conversation. They had decided that they needed another day to make a final decision about our admission.

We returned the following day. Rega Oren received us and informed us that we could enter the same week. She made a few general remarks and then pointedly observed, "You know, we're not religious; and in fact we don't have any interest in religious belief. We want you to understand that we wouldn't want any agitation on the subject."

The warning was obvious, but presented in a gentle, even friendly tone. Somehow or other, we got onto the subject of the prophets. We learned they were greatly admired by these kibbutz Socialists. Their enthusiasm, however, only applied to those points which could be squeezed into their humanist philosophy.

Two days later, we gathered our belongings and arranged for transport to Kibbutz Mizra. It was a warm May morning as we dropped our bags outside the large dining hall. There were several hundred people sitting around rows and rows of tables, eating their breakfast. Someone directed us to a table inside. Rather self-consciously but unceremoniously, we sat down in the midst of the hubbub to join in our first common meal at the settlement.

Forebears

*Haya's mother's parents,
Abraham and Hannah Leder.*

*Haya's parents,
Gertrude and Jacob Kelman.*

*Menahem's Father, Hayim Schnall
(In Israel, Menahem began using
his Hebrew name, which means
"son of Hayim.")*

*Menahem's Mother,
Rivka (Weil) Schnall.*

Immediate Family

Haya's older brothers, Bunny and identical twins Mendy (left) and Charly (right).

Haya and older sister Sally, by Sally's Florida home.

Menahem in the U. S. Army, age 19, World War II.

Haya and Menahem's wedding, July 30, 1961.

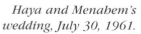

Arrival & Kibbutz Life

Haya and friend seeing her off on the ship Beer-Sheva February 7, 1963.

"Bound for the Promised Land"- Haya and Menahem on board the ship bringing them to Israel, March 1963.

Haya and Menahem in front of their wooden hut at Kibbutz Mizra.

At Kibbutz Mizra, 1963. Menahem is wearing his "tembel" hat, the typical kibbutz hat in that era.

Menahem and neighbor Gedaliah, Kibbutz Mizra.

Eilat

Haya and Menahem in their "Sing Sing" apartment in Eilat, where they lived from 1963 to 1977.

Haya, Menahem and "Bubala" behind the "Sing Sing" apartment building.

Corrie Ten Boom visits Eilat, 1970s. Menahem (rear, right) and Haya (at Corrie's left). During World War II, the Ten Boom family saved Jews in their Amsterdam, Holland, home. To Haya's left is Magda Kepesh (see Chapter 12).

Outside Eilat in the desert for a "Jewish Voice" film production, 1976.

Jerusalem

Haya and Menahem, Western Wall, 1970.

Haya and Menahem at the Menorah in front of the Knesset Building, 1970s.

Haya and Menahem at the Western Wall in Jerusalem a week or two after the Six-Day War, 1967.

Haya and Menahem, at home in Ramat Eshkol, Jerusalem, 1980s.

Haya with Israeli soldiers.

VIPs & Ministering

At the Presidential Residence, Jerusalem. Yitzchak Navon, Israel's sixth president, is speaking; Haya and Menahem are seated in the front row.

Amsterdam conference, 1986. Haya with Nigerian Christians.

Menahem and Haya speaking to a group of Japanese Christians in Jerusalem.

Menahem and Haya "with bells on" leading singing at a conference in Germany. Haya is known for her enthusiastic worship of God, whether with bells or with tambourine.

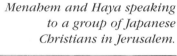

Holidays

Chanukah at the Messianic Assembly in Jerusalem. Haya and Menahem with Susie and Victor Smadja, the congregation's leader. The Benhayims have been members for many years.

Purim costumes. Menahem is reading the Esther scroll in Hebrew. Haya is Queen Esther. She loves to play dress-up!

Most Recent

March 17, 2003, Anna Ticho Restaurant, Jerusalem. Party for the fortieth anniversary of the Benhayims' aliyah. Martha and David Stern at right.

Haya and Menahem on Israel's 55th Independence Day, May 7, 2003.

Chapter Eleven

ALL THINGS COMMON

Our breakfast at the kibbutz contrasted drastically with our usual breakfast fare. It was more like a smorgasbord, with sardines, herrings, sausages, fresh vegetable salads, yogurt, cheeses, assorted jams and bread, in addition to more familiar staples like porridge and eggs. Pitchers of coffee, tea and milk were available on every table.

Breakfast was eaten at eight in the morning, after the settlers had been working physically for two or three hours. It was no doubt the meal we relished most. After a good night's rest and several hours of rigorous work in the cool of the morning, one developed a ferocious appetite.

After breakfast, we were introduced to Hava, the woman in charge of temporaries like us. She was a tall, attractive woman who spoke with a tone of voice and facial expressions which betrayed a deep weariness and added years to her appearance. Hava was always obliging and helpful and supplied us with all the necessary linens, work clothes and personal items provided by the settlement.

The living quarters assigned to us were in an outlying section of the settlement and consisted of sturdy wooden bungalows that had been partitioned into three cabin-like rooms. We took the middle room. It was furnished with two cots, a table, a simple wooden closet, one chair and a bamboo-shaded table lamp. There was a large screened window on one side of the room and a screened window leading to a porch with small wooden benches. Toilet facilities were outside our cabin in a modern cement unit a few yards to the rear. A short walk down a side path led to the settlement's swimming pool. It was a simple and cozy setup for the summer months.

The first day we spent roaming about the spacious grounds and into the nearby fields. In the evening, Hava came round to notify us of our work assignments for the following day. My husband was given work with a young man gathering bundles of cattle feed in the fields for the cowshed. I was assigned to the ironing room in the community laundry.

During our first day at work we each had a mishap. The heavy, antiquated electric iron given to me was defective. It short circuited and set the cord on fire! Out in the field, a metal rod fell on Menahem's toe while he was disengaging a cart from the tractor with which he was working. His toe swelled up, and he had to have it treated at the hospital in Afula, the nearest town. After two days, he was given a battery-driven electric cart and the job of transporting food from the main kitchen to the various children's houses. Meanwhile, we were both asked to take part in Hebrew-language studies.

Menahem already knew Hebrew quite well as a result of the considerable Jewish education he had received in his youth. This had been sustained by continued reading of the Hebrew Scriptures. Of course, he needed to learn more modern Hebrew, so he was assigned to an advanced class. Later, he told me that some of his Hebrew must have sounded to Israeli ears like the English of a foreigner who had learned his English from the King James Bible or Shakespeare's plays.

"Fantastic," one of the settlers remarked, grinning ear to

ear as Menahem innocently used some of the classical Hebrew expressions grown archaic or changed in meaning. ("Prithee, milord!" Well, it really wasn't that archaic!)

As for myself, I couldn't distinguish an "aleph"—the first letter of the Hebrew alphabet—from anything! A small group of temporary residents at the kibbutz were being given private lessons in Hebrew for a few hours each day. I was asked to join them. We were a diverse group, small as we were. My fellow students were a Swiss family of Protestants, the Roberts, from the canton of Neuchatel, who had come to join a newly-authorized Christian settlement in western Galilee called Nes Ammim.

Then there was Aviva, a young Anglo-Jewish girl from a well-to-do family in Stratford-on-Avon (the original one). The two of us could at least communicate in English, but at the time Leon Robert, his wife Jeanette and their teenage daughter Marie-Jeanne only spoke French—and the smattering of Hebrew they were picking up daily. I spoke no French whatsoever, and even less Hebrew than they did. We were often speechless.

Within a few days, Menahem and I were both fairly acclimated to the routine of communal life. We had that uncomfortable feeling experienced by many visitors that the bulk of the settlement's members were rather withdrawn. No doubt it was good that they dispensed with all the small talk of ordinary social intercourse. Greetings like "Good morning," inquiries after one's health, attempts to be interested in co-workers and neighbors, if only for the purpose of getting to know one another—all these were out. It wasn't disastrous, but for a while we felt a strain living in such close quarters with people so reserved and close-mouthed.

After a period in the laundry, I was assigned to the clean-up department. The settlement had built a lovely modern clubhouse for its members, which was open most evenings. It had to be thoroughly cleaned the following day. The floors were mopped, the furniture polished, the windows washed, the dishes and glassware scoured, and the rooms dusted and tidied up to get the place in shape for use later in the day.

When the clubhouse was not in use, I would be assigned to the orchards for fruit picking or to help out in the large community kitchen. Although I was only on a half day work schedule, the other half being devoted to Hebrew studies, I usually felt exhausted by the time the morning was over, especially after lifting and moving the furniture around the clubhouse!

My husband had his problems, too, with the improvised cart that was given him. It crawled along at a speed of about two miles an hour, if that, packed full with pots and pans and trays and bags of hot and cold food for delivery at some ten different points in the settlement three times a day. He had to weave in and out of narrow paths and avoid all kinds of cracks and bumps in the sidewalks and pathways, not to speak of the constant dread of spills at sharp turns with the wobbly, overstuffed cart. After loading and delivery, he then had to pick up the return loads at each point, deposit them in the kitchen, clean out the cart, and help with the final cleaning of the children's supply kitchen.

After several frustrating breakdowns of the cart, Menahem persuaded the work supervisor to transfer him to the fields. There he worked with the irrigation team and fruit picking. My own work schedule also changed somewhat too. Now, instead of devoting the bulk of the morning to the clubhouse, my time was divided between it and the toilets scattered about the settlement. We were kept hopping! The often impersonal atmosphere in the settlement was a challenge to us. We tried to be friendly with the members, but most of the social response came from the various groups of temporaries and visitors coming in and out of the settlement. There were student groups from France, Britain and Denmark, and sojourners from places as far off as Indonesia and New Zealand—all interested in sampling the common life.

One week, we met Muluneh, an earnest young Ethiopian Christian who had won a national Bible quiz in his homeland. His prize was an all-expenses-paid trip to Israel, the "Land of the Bible." Several weeks were devoted to life on a kibbutz. It was disconcerting for him to encounter the naked unbelief characteristic of the settlement members. We and Muluneh would get together for prayers and Bible study, and we exchanged gospel songs in English and Amharic.

For a while there was an officer in the Iranian Army staying at the settlement. He was a veterinarian taking advanced studies in poultry care. The kibbutz had developed a modern poultry plant with a three-story building for housing chickens. He listened quietly and noncommittally to us when we spoke of the Gospel in conversation. Once, he expressed annoyance at the divisiveness of religion.

"There's only one God!" he remarked, his face clouding. "I'll tell you the truth, I don't like all these religious differences." We remained friends, and he invited us to visit him in Teheran. (This was some time before the Khomeini revolution, which proved very hostile to Jews and Israel.)

We also met a young African from Basutoland in Southern Africa. He had received his education at a Christian missionary school and was a professing Anglican. "The missionaries do much good," he once told us. "But then they tell us to be submissive, and that's not good."

The settlement organized occasional study trips for groups of temporaries, providing a knowledgeable guide, food and beverages, and large trucks fitted with rows of benches for passengers. As we jostled and bounced about the hills and valleys of Galilee and along the shore of Lake Kinneret, layer upon layer of historic epochs piled up before our eyes.

There Mount Tabor rose up, where Barak, son of Abinoam, defeated the Canaanite army during the days of the judges of Israel. On the same hilltop stood a monastery erected to commemorate Yeshua's transfiguration. Lush fields and trim settlements stretched out far and wide below in the Jezreel Valley of Lower Galilee, proclaiming the presence of the returning Israelites to their ancient homeland. Nearby, lay Megiddo with its profusion of associations: *the waters of Megiddo* of Deborah's victory ode over the Canaanite hosts (Judges 5:19). Megiddo was also one of the store cities established by Solomon during the golden age of the first Hebrew commonwealth in the Holy Land, and the site of good king Josiah's tragic death in battle not long before the kingdom of Judah's final collapse. And here was Megiddon, the valley and the mountain, where the prophet Zechariah and John the revelator foresaw the climactic events at the end of the age. *"And he gathered them together in the place called in the Hebrew tongue 'Ar Megiddon"* (i.e., Mount Megiddo; Revelation 16:16).

Gradually, with the interaction of close communal life, some of the reserve of the people we worked with eased up. Gedaliah, who lived in a section near us, was an amiable man in his late thirties. He had survived the European Holocaust, immigrated to Israel and settled on the kibbutz. He was married with three small children, active in youth leadership, and a teacher of arts and crafts in the settlement school. He was also interested in improving his English, and suggested that we exchange visits using English as our medium of conversation. Well, that wasn't going to advance us in Hebrew, I could see!

Gedaliah was amazed to see us reading the New Testament on the porch and to learn that we were believers in Yeshua. "You're the first Jews I ever met who believed in Yeshua," he remarked in astonishment. He immediately pulled us over to meet his wife. "Do you know, these are Jewish people who believe in Yeshua and in the New Testament!" he exclaimed to her. She smiled, and with more typical kibbutz reserve, commented, "Well, some people are religious and some people like us aren't."

The people of the kibbutz were relatively free from the traditional Jewish prejudices towards Jews who believe in Yeshua, and were fairly tolerant of such people. This was the result of a general indifference to all religious belief. It was the kind of tolerance which people may have for matters which don't especially interest them.

Many of the kibbutz members had even read parts of the New Testament. We could see from visits to their homes that they weren't averse to displaying full Bibles on their bookshelves with the phrase *"Brit Hadasha"* ("New Testament") clearly lettered on the book's spine. These Scriptures were made available by book distributors who were anxious to put them in the hands of Jewish people everywhere. We learned from one of them that the kibbutzim often requested large quantities of full Bibles in Hebrew for their language studies. These would be presented as gifts upon completion of Hebrew language seminars. In some of their high schools, we were informed, limited study of the New Testament in Hebrew was part of the curriculum.

Like many unorthodox Jews, our neighbor Gedaliah took a sympathetic view of Yeshua and the early Christian movement. But this sympathy was fitted into his ideas about human progress. He and others like him handled the subject as they did the biblical prophets. From this perspective, primitive Christianity was an ancient landmark in the steep, ongoing ascent of humanity, but it wasn't especially relevant to Jews today.

"People in those days were like beasts!" Gedaliah remarked heatedly one day during our English discourse. "Why, look at the things they did in ancient times!" There followed a catalog of ancient cruelties he had picked up from history books. Yet it seemed strange that he should pass such sharp judgment on those of another age. He himself had lived through a period of human depravity during the Holocaust which had probably outdone all of humanity's forebears in the long history of human evil.

We would also reason with him from the Scriptures about the hand of God overruling human wickedness. He knew the prophecies, the warnings and the hopes. He had himself lived through some phases of the ancient prophetic dream of the return to Zion. Like many modern Jews, however, he couldn't reconcile the terrible cruelties of war and persecution with God's existence. We may sometimes have seemed to him like Job's comforters.

He once remarked sadly, "It's so hard not to believe. Life is hard then, especially in time of trouble."

The determination of the kibbutz settlers not to believe was sometimes pathetic, sometimes ludicrous. It was a kind of irreligious dogmatism. My husband was once speaking with a young mother in the kitchen during a break at work.

"There's no need to believe that the *Tanakh* is the word of God," she insisted. "But if it isn't," Menahem protested, "then we are thieves in the land. The Arabs would be right to claim that we have no place here."

"No, no!" she declared emphatically. "That's not so!"

"Why not?" he asked.

"Every people has a right to its own land, and this is our land," she asserted.

"But why is this our land?" Menahem persisted. "Isn't it because God promised it to us forever? And this promise is recorded in the Bible, so that the whole world may know it."

"Of course," she agreed. "The Bible is very important, very important. But it's still true that every people has its own land, and this is ours."

Another time in class, a young North African Jewish student requested a definition for the word *"ruchani"* ("spiritual"). The instructor provided a secular parable. "A man comes home from a hard day's work, sits down in his comfortable chair and reads the paper or listens to some good music. This is *'ruchani.'*"

Astonished at this illustration, Menahem commented, "And what about something like *tefillah* (prayer)?" There was a moment of pained silence and the instructor passed on to another topic.

The months passed swiftly. Menahem finished his Hebrew class and began working full time in the fields. I continued my work, with occasional assignments to fruit picking. I much preferred the atmosphere among the fruit trees to that of the privies and clubhouse!

The Hebrew New Year was approaching in late

September. I was told that I would have to sign up for a six-month stay for the new *ulpan*, the Hebrew language seminar, which would soon resume. Although Menahem was willing to stay on indefinitely, he didn't want to commit himself to a specific time period. As for myself, I'd had it!

A friend of ours, a lady distributing religious books throughout the country, invited us to stay with her on Mount Carmel. We packed our belongings, and one day Rose Warmer drove down to the settlement in her big station wagon. We made our farewells to the many people we had met during the summer. To a number of them we gave parting gifts of Scriptures.

We were invited to come back for the Hebrew New Year celebrations, which we did. It was a pleasant festive meal and entertainment in the spacious, gaily-decorated dining room. But all the spiritual meaning which traditional Judaism assigns to the Hebrew New Year—prayer, repentance and good works—had been eliminated.

The ladies under whose supervision I had worked for some time were very gracious to me. They thanked me for my assistance, and as a token of appreciation gave me a small Hebrew book as a parting gift. It was written by the wife of Israel's second President, Rachel Yannai Ben-Tzvi, and recounted her experiences as a pioneer settler during the early part of the twentieth century, describing also how she walked barefoot from Tel Aviv to Jerusalem!

Chapter Twelve

SOUTHWARD HO!

We spent some two months in Cababir, a small Arab village close to a Jewish settlement on Mount Carmel. Here Rose Warmer had made her home for many years. It was a base for her very extensive book distribution work in the Land.

Rose was certainly well equipped for her work in this multilingual country. Originally from Hungary, she had learned some fourteen languages, including Hebrew, Arabic and English. We accompanied Rose on one trip to Ashdod, the Mediterranean coastal town that was being developed on the ancient Philistine site. A new modern harbor was in the planning stage.

We were amazed at the warm response to the offer of Bibles, New Testaments and literature. My husband also has a certain flair for languages and employed all his talents. Speaking Hebrew, Yiddish, German, Spanish, English and some very fractured French, we had some exciting encounters with Zion's recently restored exiles. The people we met were, for the most part, new immigrants still going through the acute pangs of readjustment to a new and very unfinished country. The new Ashdod was only several years old at the time, and everyone living there came from somewhere else.

Back in Haifa, in late October, we had to make a decisive move. We hadn't come to a final decision about our status in Israel and were still registered as tourists. We devoted two days to prayer and fasting and studying the Scriptures.

Towards the end of a session of intense prayer, Menahem suddenly arose and abruptly announced, "Look, we have to go down to Eilat. We'll move quickly." Actually it was a move of faith. We knew that in Eilat there were a few believers and that it was a new and undeveloped town of about 5,000 people where, among a thoroughly secular population, we could fit in more easily as Messianic Jews. We took some of our personal belongings, leaving the heavier things with Rose, and made arrangements to take the bus the following morning. We arrived in Tel Aviv in time to catch the last bus down to Eilat. It was the eve of the Sabbath and no other bus was scheduled until late the following afternoon. It looked as though we might be stranded with our bags in Tel Aviv, as the ticket seller refused to issue tickets.

"Buy them on the bus, if any place is available," he told us. We ran over to the bus and were the last passengers aboard. Happily, we found two seats in the front, the only ones left. We paid our fare and settled down for a long six-and-a-half-hour journey southward through the great Negev desert.

Night had fallen when our bus pulled into the ramshackle depot located in a small town square. We had the address of a Jewish believer who ran a modest hotel at Eilat's western edge. Magda Kepesh, an immigrant from Hungary, had suffered much physically and emotionally as a result of a birth deformity. She had nevertheless marvelously survived the Nazi persecution when Jews were herded into ghettos and systematically rounded up for extermination.

After the war, Magda moved to England, where she lived in London and established a small women's lingerie shop to support herself. Then she decided that she had to come to Israel. In Haifa, where she settled, she came into contact with the Bethesda congregation of believers and eventually entered into full fellowship with them.

Some time later, she was informed by her physician that her physical condition had deteriorated and that she had but a short time to live. He recommended that she move to the dry desert climate of Eilat, where she would be more comfortable.

When we arrived in Eilat, Magda had already outlived her physician's prediction. She had been living in the town for three years and had built up a flourishing tourist business in the small two-story concrete building that she leased. We stayed a little over two weeks at Magda's, during which time we made some important decisions.

First, we decided to change our status from that of tourists to permanent residents. We applied to the Ministry of the Interior for classification as new immigrants under the Law of Return. Menahem began to inquire about job opportunities. The field was quite limited. Hospital work was not immediately available, but he could work underground as a miner. Timna, a recently discovered site, was widely believed to be part of the ancient copper mines developed by King Solomon. Now it was being turned into a modern industry. Hundreds of Jewish men were engaged in a type of work that few Jews had done since biblical times— except perhaps as prisoners or captives.

Menahem decided it was too late in life for him to go underground. He could work well above ground if he was interested in joining a construction gang. The town was booming. Blocks of apartments, shops, a new port along the shore and other structures were rising up out of the desert. In fact, a whole new town west of the present site was already on the drawing board. There was an acute shortage of skilled and unskilled labor in the town.

But it was the seashore that beckoned. There was a great demand for stevedores in the rapidly growing town, which was biding its time until the new port was ready for use. So Menahem tried his hand at stevedoring.

We had to endure only a small part of the bureaucratic shuffling for which Israel is famous. All in all, things seemed much smoother in that respect than in Haifa. There were relatively few immigrants to compete for the attention of the handful of officials serving in Eilat. The man at the Jewish Agency was especially helpful. He was a type of what seemed to be a vanishing breed—a dedicated Zionist idealist. The old pioneer chant had proclaimed: "We have come to the Land to build and to be built up within it."

Mr. Sakhrin cut through red tape with the efficiency and determination of a typical American executive. Within a few days he found us an inexpensive apartment and had all our papers set up, or in process, for our status as olim chadashim ("new immigrants"). He seemed to respect us for immigrating from the U.S. At least during one phone conversation with the housing authorities he used this fact to get things moving for us. As far as we know, we were the first immigrant couple from the U.S. to settle in Eilat.

On November 11, 1963, during our first year in Israel, we moved into our apartment on Eilat's main street, the Avenue of the Palms—only the palms were still a dream! A few days later, Menahem began work at the port. During that same week, we met a young Jewish believer who had just accepted Yeshua while serving in the Israeli army.

Baruch Maoz had been born in the United States. When he was eleven, his mother had immigrated to Israel with her two young sons. Baruch spoke flawless Hebrew and considered himself an Israeli rather than an American. For a while, he was in a youth group that founded Kibbutz Eilot, some three kilometers north of Eilat. It was Israel's southernmost communal settlement.

Baruch—or Ricky, as everyone called him—had had a stormy adolescence and was like an unbridled maverick. In Eilat, he came into contact with a Gentile family of Pentecostals from South Africa who preached the Gospel to him over a period of a year and a half. The head of the family, an Afrikaaner, was an ardent Zionist and an experienced miner who had become a shift boss at the Timna Mines.

About the time we came down to Eilat, Baruch had an encounter with Obadiah, another maverick soul. Obadiah was a dark young Yemenite Jew who had grown up in Trinidad, and spoke English with a typical West Indies lilt. When his family moved to Israel, Obadiah developed into an outspoken believer in Yeshua—to put it mildly! His outspokenness was just too much for the Israel Defense Forces into which he had been inducted. He refused to salute officers or address them as *ham'fakedd* ("Sir"). When asked why, he would answer, "God is my *m'fakedd*." He spoke constantly about Yeshua. He was finally discharged as unsuited to military service.

Now the IDF is a veritable melting pot of world Jewry's regathered children and normally quite tolerant of a variety of shades of religious and political beliefs. Jewish believers have served, and continue to serve, in the army, some having attained to officer rank. In the army, Obadiah and Baruch met and clashed—and the resultant release of spiritual energy catapulted Baruch from being a determined atheist to being a zealous believer in Yeshua. It was one of those rare conjunctures which defy logical patterns. Both of them were the most unlikely people to act upon or to be acted upon in the ordinary categories of faith and experience. But then, can the spiritual world be confined to ordinary categories of faith—or experience?

After completing his initial military service, Baruch settled in Eilat and joined the small Eilat congregation. At first, we met every Saturday night in Magda's downstairs flat for worship and preaching. Frequently, there were visitors—Israelis and non-Israelis, believers and inquirers. Beginning with Baruch, five young local Israelis joined the fellowship, each one led by his friend.

We were speaking quite openly about our faith. Menahem was soon known as a believer in Yeshua. A number of local people professed to believe and even joined in fellowship. Many came to meetings. We were conducting three a week—one for prayer, one for witness and one for celebration of the Lord's supper among the believers.

Life in Eilat was very much the life of a frontier town. I remember—before the program of desalination of water went into effect—how we got our drinking water. Twice a week a water truck would circuit our area. The driver would hop out of the cabin and shake a noisy clanging cowbell. The whole neighborhood erupted as we rushed out and gathered around the spigot of the big, blimpish tank. We thrust out our jerrycans, pots, pans, buckets—anything that could hold water—and filled them up with crystal clear, distilled water. The ordinary water that flowed from our taps was so hard and heavy with magnesium and other minerals that it was more than likely to give one a good case of stomach cramps or diarrhea. (Of course, it was adequate for mopping floors and flushing the toilet!) Good drinking water was a top priority during the blistering summer days, when daily temperatures sometimes rose well above 100° F (about 40° C).

Yet there was a rugged beauty to the natural desert landscape, which compensated for some of its starker qualities. After sunset, when the Edom hills to the east were transformed by the stunning shades of the afterglow, I half expected a possé of horsemen to trot out of the hills. Not too long after our arrival, a prefabricated "Wild West" set was created a few miles southwest of the town for producing films—the so-called "spaghetti Westerns." Later, I also worked as a costumed extra in some of these.

Eilat was known as the "end-of-the-world" town. A few short miles to the east, across the bay, lay Aqaba, famed for the exploits of Lawrence of Arabia. It was within walking distance—except that to do so would be risking life and limb along the well-guarded border of a then enemy nation, the Hashemite Kingdom of Jordan. A little further south, along the eastern side of the bay, stretched the vast Arabian wasteland. To the south of us, again in walking distance, was the Egyptian border and the expanses of the Sinai desert.

Only to the north, in the howling waste of wilderness of the biblical Exodus (Deuteronomy 32:10), lay the Negev desert to which the Eilati could turn for breathing space and elbow room. A handful of settlements dotted Israel's largest land mass. Eilat was the only sizeable town between the Red Sea and Beersheva, 150 miles to the north, along a rough, hazardous road. During times of border tension, the latter had claimed many lives, as murderous gangs of the so-called Arab fedayeen ("fighters") waylaid travelers between the two points.

The townspeople were a diverse mosaic of humanity. Many were new immigrants, predominantly from Middle

Eastern countries. There were adventurers, and not a few "Australian-type" settlers. These were chronic lawbreakers who, in the early days of settlement, had been given the option of "exile" to Eilat or to prison in the north. There were Israelis who came to stay for a few years, earn high wages, and benefit from the many tax and wage incentives offered settlers at Israel's "end of the world."

The great youth migration, which was evolving into the worldwide "hippie" movement, was also drawing considerable numbers of young people into the town. The climate was ideal for inexpensive living in improvised huts on the beaches and in the wadis near Eilat. The cry for casual, unskilled labor was so strong that even those with tourist visas were grabbed up by hotels, restaurants and contractors, all hungry for workers. Eventually, it became perfectly legal to employ tourists in Eilat, and the local Labor Exchange began to handle them routinely.

Many young Jews from Western countries were attracted to the town as temporary residents. The Jewish Agency gave them three years in which to decide whether they would become permanent residents.

Chapter Thirteen

BY THE SHORES OF THE RED SEA

"That's a sweet little pup you have, Ma'am," our tall blondish neighbor Arieh commented one afternoon. We had been living in Eilat for a few months. Our small dog, whom we called "Bubala," was snowy white in the greater part of his small body, with brooding black patches and stripes on his head and torso. Temperamentally like a child, he was completely devoted to us.

The treatment of animals in Israel leaves much to be desired. The negative attitude held by many Middle Eastern people towards dogs and cats has left its mark. The Bible speaks of future bliss in the animal kingdom: *The wolf shall dwell with the lamb ... and they shall not hurt or destroy in all my holy mountain"* (Isaiah 11:6, 9). And I always tried to help the kingdom along a bit. In the big family house we had in Connecticut when I was growing up, and in our summer cottage, we had a private menagerie. At one time, we had two dogs, two cats, canaries, lovebirds and a bowl of goldfish.

In our little flat in Eilat, we were quite restricted for space. While we kept the dog at home, we "raised" several generations of cats outside on the porch and in the backyard, and fed a variety of vagrant birds and pigeons. I also took care not to destroy the melodious crickets that occasionally found shelter in our bathroom. They provided a real country flavor at night during the warm weather, with their shrill, metallic chatter.

One of our neighbors raised poultry for a while in her yard, which added musical color to the surroundings, among other things. The motley crowds of dogs and cats roaming the town and its outskirts added to the impression of a lively animal suburbia. This was supplemented by the establishment of a zoo by an old German Jewish veterinarian not far from the sea. It was supposed to be an extension of Jerusalem's biblical zoo—but it often floundered for lack of funds and staff. We also had a maritime museum in town to display the dazzling and lavishly-colored underwater life swarming in the Red Sea.

My love of animals often led to interesting encounters with neighbors. We established a lasting friendship with the delightful Israeli couple whose bitch sired our pet "Bubala." Although they were devoted to the basic principles of Judaism they were completely free of prejudice towards our New Covenant faith.

Our neighbor Arieh also became quite friendly. He would often visit us after work and bring along extra food for Bubala from the hotel kitchen where he worked. Then he announced that he was visiting Haifa, and asked us for the names and addresses of other believers up north. He decided to take a young friend, Ami, to a gospel meeting at Bethesda Hall in Haifa.

The son of German-Jewish immigrants, Ami had been born in Israel and raised without any religious faith by agnostic parents. Something in the simple gospel meeting moved Ami. It was extremely rare for a Jewish person in Israel to respond to the Gospel message at the first hearing. By a miracle of grace, Ami did, and soon entered into fellowship with the local believers. Arieh also made a profession of faith after many hearings, but eventually dropped out of sight.

One man from America who was about to return to the States after a period as a temporary resident became so furious at our testimony of faith that he tore the shirt off Menahem's back and started screaming like a madman.

On a bus trip north, we became friendly with a musician with whom Menahem reasoned quietly about spiritual matters. It appears that he had once professed Yeshua as the Messiah but eventually had renounced his decision. No arguments ensued nor were harsh words exchanged. Suddenly, his face clouded and in a frenzy he turned to his neighbor, a young Gentile traveling with him, and shrieked, "These people are Christians!" Then he began hurling obscenities and vile language at us. It was like something one reads about in mythology, a man suddenly turning into a beast.

We're not psychologists or exorcists. There are people who are disturbed, and some who are demonic. One never knows when some word will arouse the worst in them. These are the exceptions that put the rule to the test; the rule that normally people said, "You believe what you want to. If we want to hear, you can tell us and we'll listen. But don't 'bug' us."

There were other kinds of exceptions, like Bill. His father a Scotsman, his mother an Englishwoman who was Jewish, Bill had been raised in "Progressive" Judaism. From the time we first met him, after he had been fired from a job at the port, he kept traveling back and forth between the U.K. and Israel in five attempts to settle in Israel.

He would spend hours with us, attend meetings of the local believers and ask us to pray for him. But it always ended up, "I believe in Progressive Judaism. We don't need

Yeshua as our atonement." In Israel, his Judaism seemed to be "progressively" diminishing as he rejected more and more of the Hebrew Scriptures, the Tanakh.

On the whole, we had good relations with our neighbors, many of whom were from Middle Eastern lands. They were puzzled by us but never hostile. We were often invited to wedding feasts, circumcisions, bar mitzvahs and ordinary social visits. One often needed to have a sense of humor and an appreciation for the colorful splashes of the human comedy-drama being enacted, of which we ourselves were part. In a town like Eilat and a country like Israel, something of both is always near at hand.

One of our close neighbors was Miriam. She had lived for a month in Paris en route to Israel from her native Morocco and insisted on calling herself a Frenchwoman! There was prejudice in Israel against Moroccan Jews. She was convinced that by identifying herself as a Frenchwoman, she would have greater status, especially in our eyes, her "high-born" American neighbors. Actually, for us it was quite exotic and interesting to meet Jews from the Middle East, about which we had had little firsthand knowledge in America.

Miriam had recently married a thin, nervous Moroccan Jew, a tailor, some fifteen years her senior. This was shortly after her arrival in Israel, and our Hebrew was just about on the same level, so Miriam and I didn't feel ill at ease conversing haltingly to one another. The following year, she had her first child, Osnat, and during the first summer of her life, Osnat became seriously ill. Dehydration, the doctors said —nothing serious—just keep feeding her fluids.

But Osnat grew worse, and finally had to be admitted to the local hospital, whose facilities were quite limited at the time. For a while, her life hung in the balance, and she was flown up north for treatment. Miriam wouldn't leave her side, sleeping on a bench or vacant bed. We visited with her at the hospital in the north, and prayed earnestly with her. At her request, we spoke to the doctors, who insisted that there was no need for her to stay there day and night. But she was determined not to forsake her child even for a minute. And Osnat did pull through.

About a year later, a similar incident took place in another neighboring family. An infant of six weeks was taken ill and brought to the local clinic. Again, the diagnosis of mild dehydration—not serious—but during the night her condition grew worse. The baby was taken to the hospital and admitted. By morning, she had gasped out her last breath.

At 5 A.M., we were awakened by a pounding on the door. Our neighbor, a young man who had come to Israel from Romania as a child, entered sobbing, "She's gone, the girl is gone!"

"What's happened? What's happened?" we asked in amazement and shock. Then the wife came in, a young woman originally from North Africa. She was hysterical.

We read with them from the opening chapter of the book of Job, with its poignant description of Job receiving the tragic news of his children's death. It had some effect in quieting the couple.

My husband went around with the distraught father to help make the final arrangements. Because the child was still an infant, the religious authorities ruled that no religious rites could be permitted. The little body was wrapped up in a cloth. My husband and I and one friend of the family were asked to accompany them to the cemetery. There, the rabbinical official slid the body down into an open pit, covered her, and uttered not a word—neither prayer, nor Scripture, nor words of comfort. As if the loss of an infant child is not anguish enough to parents. Fortunately, they were a young couple, and in a few years they had two healthy sons.

Menahem wondered why I didn't get pregnant after five years of marriage. When I went for tests, I was told the reason I hadn't conceived was that I had a large vaginal tumor. It needed operating on urgently. It was a major operation that took most of the day. The hospital at that time was a very small 21-bed prefabricated building. Although the tumor wasn't malignant, the operation turned into a hysterectomy! I had a very painful and difficult recovery. I was in the hospital for two weeks, during which time I was able to witness for the Lord and give out Bibles in different languages.

The head nurse told me that it would be better if I didn't take any medication, so the pain was severe. I noticed that if I spoke of our faith I forgot about the pain, and when I stopped it came back again! The doctors, nurses, patients and even visitors received the Scriptures—I think because I looked so pathetic and weak they were afraid that if they didn't take them I might collapse!

We met the night nurse again in Haifa when we were visiting the city a year after the operation. She was taking a course there to be a visiting nurse. She told me I was their best patient (I think because I could hardly talk or walk for the two weeks I was in the hospital). She also had received a Bible.

Meanwhile, in the easygoing environment of Eilat there were basic unsettled moral issues that sometimes sapped the life of the assembly. We discovered there was an unrepentant adulterer who was professing to believe, and held himself up as a leader and teacher in the congregation. A spirit of

bitterness and recrimination among several local believers
time and again caused strife and confusion. The rashness of
youthful zeal among new believers added to the tensions.

For a while it was getting so bad that I felt we should
separate ourselves from the group. My husband was
adamant. We must work from within the group. We must
not start another group. Finally, the regular fellowship
came to an end of itself, as most of the people left town in
the ongoing flux of frontier life. And we were left just a
handful of believers. Though we were but a handful, we
continued to share our faith. There were always new
people passing through.

We had a number of film festivals in our home. Films
were lent to us by various people in Israel. They dealt with
Israel, prophecy, the Bible and science, and the like.
Sometimes we also had guests who provided a link with the
larger world of believers. Corrie Ten Boom visited once. She
was a Dutch Christian who, with her family, was part of the
Dutch resistance movement to rescue Jews during the
German occupation of Holland. Four members of her family
perished at the hands of the Nazis during World War II. After
the war, her family was honored by Yad Vashem, the
Holocaust Memorial Museum, on the Avenue of the
Righteous Gentiles, in Jerusalem. It was a moving meeting as
she shared her experience and faith with us.

Roy Gustafson and his wife, working with the Holy Land
Tours of the Billy Graham Foundation visited with us. Ken
Anderson, an evangelical Christian film producer, explored with
us the possibility of making a Hebrew film about the life of
Messianic believers in Israel. But at the time, many Israeli
Jewish believers were reluctant to expose themselves to
possible harassment by zealots in the wake of such a film.

People with a burden for Israel and her prophetic destiny stopped by, individually and in groups. They came from every part of the world.

Barring a few incidents, we found a relatively tolerant attitude towards believers among the townspeople. They weren't especially tradition-minded. There were so many flagrant violations of Jewish tradition in town that only the hardiest or most accommodating religious Jews would settle there. Those who did tended to be more tolerant and meek. For a while, we even had several friends among the religious young people, and a few among the older traditionalists, with whom we had friendly dialogues about the Messiah and the New Testament. For the most part, they came and left after relatively brief sojourns.

Whether by word of mouth, by deed or by our lives, we wanted to share in the renewal of Israel in the ancient homeland. We trusted God that He who was restoring Hebrew national life would restore it spiritually as well. And we who had experienced the firstfruits of that spiritual restoration were called, in patience and in hope, to be a part of this great renewal.

Long ago, Paul, the Hebrew apostle to the Gentiles, had expressed his hope concerning Israel's final deliverance: *"What will their acceptance [of Yeshua] mean but life from the dead?"* (Romans 11:15).

We were part of that hope.

Chapter Fourteen

RUMORS AND WAR

The news media were full of reports on the latest crisis. U.N. troops were withdrawing from the Sinai Peninsula. Egyptian troops were pouring in. Israeli forces were mobilizing.

One afternoon in mid-May, 1967, a neighbor stopped in. Gilda, a tall, red-haired nurse, had had a rather checkered life. Her father, a German Jewish lawyer, had moved to Scotland after the rise of the Nazis. There he settled down and married a Scotswoman. Gilda was a restless young woman who had moved in a variety of circles. At the moment, she was living with an Israeli lawyer who thought we were oddballs. Before they had teamed up, she used to visit and discuss the Bible with us. But lately she shied away from us. Her escort preferred that she stay off religious topics, she told us.

"Nasser has closed the Straits of Tiran," she announced somberly after she sat down. "There will be war." (Although the Straits were an international waterway, Nasser had closed them to Israeli shipping.)

Tension was mounting, and my husband was anxiously seeking an answer about what we should do.

"I'm going to have our dog put to sleep," Gilda informed us. "There'll be a siege, and no food." She spoke almost as if she were intoning an oracle.

"Well," my husband countered, "a dog can surely manage by himself even in a siege. There's no need to put him down."

"You don't understand," she continued melodramatically.

"If there's a siege, people will be famished. They'll kill the dogs for food. You don't know these people!"

I was stupefied by her statements. I couldn't believe that the situation could get so bad. Meanwhile, tourists had abandoned the town. Many families were being sent up north, even some wives of officials in the municipality—to the dismay of those left behind. The only outsiders visible were television and media crews from Europe and North America.

"It's the number one story in Europe," a correspondent in town told Menahem. "Something has got to break."

More and more men were being called up for military service. Menahem went down to the town Major and offered to serve. "You could lose your U.S. citizenship," he was told. "You can't go." At that time the U.S. did not permit dual nationality for its citizens. "What about volunteer work?" he asked. He was referred to an emergency volunteer group being organized in case of an attack on the town. He would be in a first-aid squad since he had been a medic during World War II.

Meanwhile, he worked with a construction gang, which was quickly reshuffled to build improvised emergency shelters and defense walls against shrapnel and air raid attacks.

Then Nasser told the world that Eilat was in Israeli hands illegally and should be Arab territory. We were blockaded by the sea and sealed in by the Sinai desert to the south, with hostile neighbors to the east. Only the Negev—for the most part a vast unsettled desert to the north—was still free. There could be no doubt that every attempt would be made to sever Eilat from the rest of Israel. Eilat would then be strangled, and in more ways than one. Nasser had employed poison gas in his recent war with Yemen. If he could use

such a weapon against his Arab "brethren," why should he
hesitate to use it against "illegal" Eilat?

Menahem decided to inquire about moving me up north.
He phoned friends in Jerusalem and Haifa, just in case, and
then we had our own council of war.

"No," I told him, "If you stay, I stay."

Later, he told me my decision reminded him of a wife on
the Titanic. Faced with the choice of abandoning her
husband, Isadore Strauss, to join the women and children in
the lifeboats, Mrs. Ida Strauss had turned back. "After all
these years together, I'm not leaving you now, Isadore," she
had declared, and they went down together with the ill-
fated vessel.

Eilat was beginning to feel like the Titanic. We had the
eerie feeling of people living on the edge of a precipice, and
leaning over dangerously. What the next day, the next hour
would bring, no one knew. We were told to tape up the
windows to prevent broken glass, and the town was blacked
out every night.

The tension kept up until Israel's pre-emptive strike in
early June. Abroad, feverish negotiating, politicking,
demonstrating and counter-demonstrating were taking place.
There was a steady flow of reports and rumors. One
morning, I felt an agonizing burden, as if the end were near.
I tried to dismiss it as a normal response to the uncertainty
of the crisis. But it persisted, and I went on my knees in
prayer in the bedroom with great heaviness of heart for us
and the people of Eilat, for well over an hour. I don't think I
ever prayed so intensely, until the burden lifted.

Monday morning, Menahem came home for breakfast after
the all-clear signal in what we thought had been an air-raid
drill. As I opened the door, a neighbor came down the stairs.

He worked in the Timna copper mine outside of Eilat.

"What's the news?" I asked.

"War. It's already begun in Gaza," he replied briefly.

"So that wasn't just a drill," my husband remarked.

Soon an army truck started moving through the town. A loudspeaker announced that all men who had not yet been mobilized and were in the reserve forces should report immediately to the Town Major or to their regular units.

Women were again weeping as their menfolk— husbands, sons and brothers—were off again in Israel's seemingly endless round of wars. But there was no hysteria. Wherever they were building shelters, the women and children would help, loading buckets with sand and gravel, bringing out drinks for the workers, inviting them to their homes to listen to the brief hourly news bulletins on the radio. There was again a widespread spirit of fraternity and mutual helpfulness.

On the first day of the war there were two air raid alerts. We rushed excitedly into the improvised shelters. At night, there was a total blackout of Eilat and Aqaba in Jordan. As if by some magic wand, two glittering towns on opposite sides of the bay suddenly vanished in the darkness.

Early on the morning of the second day of the war, a command car filled with Israeli troops raced through the main street. The few people out on the street waved happily to them as the soldiers sang cheerful Hebrew songs. We had all just heard the astonishing news of the tremendous Israeli air strikes that had demolished the enemy air forces of Jordan, Egypt, Iraq and Syria while they were still on the ground. The worst of the tension was gone. We knew victory would be ours, but were as yet unaware of its staggering dimensions.

First, the Egyptian armies were driven back through the

Sinai Desert and across the Suez Canal—for the second time in twenty years. Then East Jerusalem, Judea and Samaria were restored to Jewish sovereignty for the first time in 2,000 years. And finally, on the last day of the war, the Syrians were driven from the Golan Heights, from which they had been ceaselessly harassing Israeli settlements in the valley below for twenty years.

From different parts of the world, believers wrote to us, recalling Yeshua's words in the Gospel of Luke, *"Jerusalem will be trodden down by the Gentiles, until the times of the Gentiles are fulfilled"* (Luke 21:24). Many wondered if the times of the Gentiles had ended or were drawing to a close.

After six days, the war was over. There were no victory celebrations, for Israeli wars, even great victories, take a great toll. Soldiers began returning home. They went back to their jobs and families, and mourned those who would not return.

Some of our neighbors who had fled to Jerusalem before the war broke out returned shamefacedly. They had had to spend some three days in underground shelters. At the time, they hadn't dreamed that Jerusalem would be heavily shelled while Eilat would be spared, not even one shot fired.

There were Israelis who had been unbelievers and scoffers before the war who returned home contrite and chastened. "Now I believe there's a God," confessed a particularly blatant infidel. Moshe, a Yemenite Jew who had turned bitterly away from Judaism in his youth, remarked, "You wouldn't believe that I could read from the prayer book and Psalms over and over and cuddle them to my heart. But that's what I did during those days."

He had been on guard duty facing the enemy across the Bay. Daily, they expected to be thrown into a life-and-death struggle with Jordanian and Egyptian forces. For some reason, although Jordan fought intensely and bravely along large sections of her border with Israel, she chose to keep the Eilat front quiet. And Israel kept it that way too.

To the south of Eilat, two hundred Egyptian tanks were lined up for a breakthrough to Aqaba in a combined Arab assault to sever Eilat from the rest of Israel. Suddenly, the enemy redeployed forces at the outbreak of hostilities. A town councillor remarked to his father-in-law, "I was an atheist until I saw how Eilat was spared. They had all those tanks lined up against us. Suddenly they moved away. It was a miracle. How could we have stood up to them?"

Many told stories of miracles, of mighty deliverances. For a short while, it seemed a new spirit was being infused into many of God's stiffnecked people. We were all grateful for the relatively few casualties sustained by Israel's armed forces. Yet it was enough to know of the tragedy of one young life snuffed out for us to refrain from glorying in the war's victory.

"Have you heard about Raffie?" someone asked us.

Raffie was a young married man whose wife was the daughter of a Jewish believer. They were very open and friendly to us when we met them shortly after they decided to settle in Eilat. We often visited with one another and with their friends. They were part of a young, outgoing, good-natured crowd living a rather bohemian lifestyle. We could talk freely about the Lord among them.

"I've passed by their apartment a number of times," Menahem remarked to a friend. "The last time we saw Raffie was just a few days before the war broke out. He still hadn't been called up. But it's been dark in their apartment every time I pass by."

"It will always be dark," came our friend's solemn reply.

"What happened?"

"Raffie died in Gaza while administering first aid to a wounded comrade. They were both killed."

We went to visit Raffie's bereaved parents as soon as we could. They were utterly broken. Nothing we could say was of comfort to them. They were of a traditional religious background, and trying to lift them a little from an almost catatonic grief, we reminded them of the words of Job, *"The Lord gave and the Lord has taken away"* (Job 1:21).

"The Lord?" was the mother's bitter reply. "It was a bullet that took away Raffie's life."

Chapter Fifteen

AFTERMATH

We scrambled ashore from the double-decked glass-bottom boat which had carried us south on the Red Sea. Scattering in all directions, a group of Israelis began exploring the little island which earlier that month had been Egyptian territory. It was called Djazirat Faraun—Isle of the Pharaohs.

Some thought it might be the ancient biblical harbor of Ezion-geber, where the fleets of Solomon and the kings of Israel found haven in their ancient shipping ventures. During the Crusades, a fortress had been built on the tiny island—320 meters long and 150 meters wide. The crumbling ruins still provided a commanding view of the bay. For us, it was Coral Island, a treasure trove of natural coral and sea life that ringed the isle like a belt.

Within a matter of days after the war's end, Israelis were clamoring to see the exotic desert territories that lay southward. The primitive dirt road that linked Eilat to the Straits of Tiran and Sharm-a-Sheikh soon felt the heavy tread of command cars, trucks, jeeps and other rough-riding vehicles that could be obtained to explore the fantastic landscape.

Soon afterwards, we took a vacation and went north to visit Jerusalem. There the glory of Israel had once dwelt, and there it had been laid in the dust more than once, judged by God and man. For the first time, after nineteen years of Jordanian occupation, Jews were streaming in the thousands into the Old City on pilgrimage to the ancient Western

(Wailing) Wall, the site of Solomon and Herod's Temples. We went by foot with a group of Jewish believers, picking our way over the rubble and debris still largely uncleared from the recent war.

We traveled about the West Bank of the Jordan River, Bethlehem, Hebron—the places which for a generation had been sealed off from Israel. There was an excitement in the air, a feeling that a new era had begun. Jews and Christians were citing the biblical prophecies. "Is it near? Is it at the door? The consummation? Is He near? Is He at the door, the longed-for Redeemer of Israel?"

Back in Eilat, things were returning to normal. People were slipping back into the routine of daily living. The dreamlike haze of a miracle was wearing off. The blistering summer heat was in full force. It was our fifth summer in Israel, and Menahem's third job working out in the gruelling heat. He had worked successively as a stevedore, as a gardener and as a building worker.

Then a friend told us about a job opening in a local shipping office at the port. It would be out of the sun. It required a good command of English and Hebrew. No problem about that, but Menahem wasn't too excited about going into office work. He still clung to romantic ideas about being a Jewish laborer building up the homeland. We prayed about it, and decided that he should at least go for the interview.

The manager of the office was an Orthodox Jewish man who wore the traditional skullcap to indicate his adherence to Jewish tradition. The subject of faith didn't come up in the interview. Menahem knew that if he volunteered it, he would almost certainly be disqualified from the start. He decided to wait and see.

Soon afterwards, he received an urgent call to start work at once. It wasn't too long before the grapevine was buzzing. In the eyes of many townspeople we were stamped as professional missionaries. This was by no means complimentary in Israel.

A few months after beginning work, Menahem spoke with the manager about filling a more challenging position opening up in the office. He met with some vague remarks about his unsuitability for the particular opening. Menahem pressed further.

"Could you tell me if there is some other reason?" he asked point blank.

The manager lowered his head, smiled and seemed embarrassed, as if hesitating to discuss the subject.

"Well, I'll tell you. I've heard rumors. I haven't had an opportunity to check them out; but anyway, I've heard rumors about you and your wife."

"What have you heard?"

"I've heard that you and your wife—or at least your wife—is a full-time paid missionary. Now, I know you understand that for me there's absolutely no place in this country for missionaries—even if this whole business was once a Jewish affair long ago! I can tell you that I was astounded, shocked, to hear that someone working in my office might be connected with missions. I don't think I could tolerate anyone representing our company who has such connections."

"Well," Menahem replied, "that we believe in the New Testament and that we are Messianic Jews is something we haven't kept a secret. This is what we sincerely believe. But we aren't employed by any mission, neither I nor my wife."

There followed an inconclusive discussion about Judaism

and missions and observance of tradition. Then the manager told Menahem he would think it over, but he wasn't convinced by his explanations. It looked like the ax would fall any day.

We later learned that there was an immediate attempt to discharge Menahem, but the office was so desperately understaffed that the supervisor of his department persuaded the manager to keep him on. He told the manager, "In Tangiers [his place of birth] we Jews got along very well with the Christians." Eventually, the manager moved on to another town, but he had been reconciled to our presence. He later invited us to the circumcision of his son.

Our little flat continued to be a crossroads of humanity. I was kept busy enough entertaining visitors. Following the war in 1967, our visitors became more diverse than ever. We might have turbaned Sikh Indians or Japanese students, European hippies or Sinai Beduin youth and visitors from black Africa—alongside our Jewish guests who were themselves a cross-section of the world.

A family of seven from the U.S. who had sailed to Israel from California on a homemade yacht stayed with us for several days. A young man preparing to translate Scripture for a small group of Aborigines in the British Solomon Islands was a guest. There was a family headed for Burundi to do Christian teaching who were stranded in Eilat without fare as a result of misinformation about sailing possibilities from the port. We helped them find work and fellowship until their family could send them the air fare to continue on to Africa.

We continued to have weekly meetings, moving about from house to house among the few believers living in town. Sometimes we would be as many as fifteen or twenty crowded into a tiny apartment for fellowship. But people came and went. We often felt acutely the sense of reality expressed by the writer of the letter to the Hebrews: *"Here we have no lasting city ..."* (Hebrews 13:14).

Sometimes, we would have an influx of visitors and I would be constantly on the go preparing meals, fixing up the house for overnight guests, taking people around town. Other times, it seemed no one was coming around, not even friends and neighbors in town.

There was always enough tension in the Middle East to keep our minds from being too preoccupied with our own problems. Our Arab "neighbors" helped us feel that we were being noticed. After the Six Day War, new terrorist groups mushroomed in the neighboring lands like weeds in summer. They often fought among themselves bitterly, and succeeded in destroying many more Arabs than Jews. It's not that Israelis are so exceptionally united, but for the most part they keep their infighting a few crucial degrees below the boiling point.

There were Arab attempts to sabotage various installations in or near town—with very little success. The roads were mined from time to time. On a few occasions shells were lobbed over from across the bay.

One morning, during the Passover festival, when Eilat was crowded with thousands of Israeli tourists from the north, many sleeping on the beaches, we were awakened at 4:00 A.M. by the booming of explosions. For almost an hour, some thirty Russian-made katyusha shells zoomed over our head, landing in various parts of town. We huddled together in our bedroom. Many of the shelters had never been completed following the lightning victories of the Six Day War. The shells tore into the streets, the exploding fragments peppering the walls and pavements. A group of cars was hit, the fuel tanks ignited and set them on fire. Yet not one person was seriously injured.

The building in which we had been living for 14 years was becoming more and more run-down. It seemed to us to be a blunder to build 112 apartments so close together at the edge of the vast Negev desert so sparsely populated. They were double-tiered so that the rear section had little benefit of the beautiful vistas of desert, sea and mountains—looking out only on backyards and sloppily-built bungalows and other monotonous prefabricated apartment blocks.

The townsfolk, half-amused and half-disdainful, dubbed it the "Railroad Train"—and then settled on the name "Sing Sing"—the famed penitentiary on the Hudson—a reference to the iron railings connecting the front and rear sections. The many young couples who moved into the small one-bedroom flats soon felt the pressure to leave as families grew. An increasing number of contractors, hotelkeepers, and industrial companies bought up or subleased the apartments. They installed their workers in ever-changing groups. Several underworld characters set up a gambling den. Sometimes drug-using youth took over apartments, wandering in and out of the country.

My husband says I have a gift for striking up a conversation with strangers. Spiritually, it proved very helpful in scattering the seed of the Word in our rough desert field. To the west of the town, a whole new area had developed. Gradually, most of the original tenants of our block moved into the newer areas. These were apartments that had to be purchased. The down payments were high and monthly payments exorbitant. Priority was given to those with young children.

We sometimes felt that we were in a revolving door, with neighbors coming and going so rapidly we barely got to know some of them by name. For a while, we succeeded in forming a neighborhood committee with the help of a few interested parties. For some years, it helped provide extra services and stirred a little community life. But interest quickly waned, and neighbors changed even more quickly. We always ended up as a committee of three or four among the several hundred inhabitants of the block.

Yet we felt for the time being that this was God's place for us. There was no difficulty here in identifying with the medieval poet Chaucer's "Ballade of Good Counsel":

Here is no home, here is but wilderness
Forth, pilgrim, forth . . .
And truth shall make you free.

Chapter Sixteen

UP TO JERUSALEM

All in all, we spent fourteen years in Eilat. Once the tensions decreased over our unusual and uncommon beliefs (at least for Jews), Menahem settled in nicely with the shipping company that employed him. From time to time he was approached by friends to be the tenth man to complete a minyan (synagogue quorum), the reason being that they needed a man to join in the kaddish prayer on the memorial day for a deceased family member. This was an indication that they still regarded him as a "kosher" Jew. His experience in the Diaspora had been that Orthodox Jews would not include him in a minyan, although they would not ask him to leave the synagogue. By this time, both Menahem and I were well known as open believers in Yeshua. We didn't feel the acute sense of rejection in Eilat that we were to experience later in Jerusalem.

In 1976, Menahem was asked to serve as the Israel secretary for the International Messianic Jewish Alliance. It was to be a temporary, part-time appointment, with a small monthly honorarium. After morning prayer, when the offer was made, he was inclined to reject it, and wrote a letter to that effect. But he left the letter unmailed, and by evening, having mulled the matter over during the day, he had gotten the clear impression that he should accept the offer. He therefore composed another letter, this time of acceptance.

Meanwhile, Menahem had begun writing articles in his

spare time as a freelancer for English language publications abroad, news reports about Israel for general readers and for Messianic Jewish and Christian readers. We began to feel that being located in Eilat, far from the hub of the country, was restrictive for both writing and serving the Israeli Messianic Jewish community. Bus travel was long and wearing; the nearest city, Beersheva, was four hours away; Tel Aviv was six, Haifa and the north even longer. We continued several more months in Eilat but then decided to move to Jerusalem.

It was not an easy decision. We were no longer young. Menahem had a good job and friendly colleagues. We had congenial neighbors and good fellowship with the small group of local believers, including John and Judy Pex, who had recently settled in the town. They were soon to become the main center for believers in Eilat, and their bold outreach continues to this day.

I was particularly pleased to learn that it had been through reading the Gospel of John in a Bible I had given to a next door neighbor that John Pex had committed his life to the Lord. He met and married Judy. Both had come to love Eilat and settled down to raise a family while ministering to the many hippies who were flooding Eilat at the time. They ran a hostel that has proved to be a spiritual opening to young people of many backgrounds, Jewish and Gentile.

In 1977, we moved to Jerusalem, but with mixed feelings. It was September, and we had to find a flat in competition with the masses of students beginning or resuming their studies at the Hebrew University of Jerusalem. We avoided ultra-Orthodox neighborhoods, knowing that even secular Jews were harassed in them if they tried to find housing there, because of their indifference to the strict Sabbath observance and moral codes that prevailed in the Orthodox surroundings. Sabbath meant no automobile travel, no loud blaring radios or televisions, and certainly no mixed male and female parties. The moral code demanded that no unmarried women visitors could come to their flats, no bikinis or other immodest dress was allowed. The newspapers occasionally reported violence inflicted on those who disregarded this code. How much more opposition could Jewish believers in Yeshua expect to find if they attempted to settle in a *haredi* (ultra-Orthodox) neighborhood. Messianic Jews were stigmatized in the Orthodox media and on posters as "dangerous missionaries" to be completely shunned.

We eventually settled in a flat in northeast Jerusalem, where we lived for nine years. At the same time the Alliance rented an office in a large downtown building. Some of the office neighbors, we later learned, complained to the management about the Alliance presence. There were attempts to break in, the nameplate on the door was defaced and graffiti scrawled on the door. From time to time, angry Orthodox Jews came in to vent their rage at the presence of Messianic Jews. A few came in out of curiosity, wanting to know what "Messianic Jews" meant.

One ultra-Orthodox Jew, on learning what we believed, entered the office and began shouting and cursing, wishing that the office would go up in flames, with Menahem in it. Menahem moved the conversation into Yiddish, the language that most Ashkenazi *haredim* speak and which Menahem had spoken from childhood. This softened the man, and before long he was trying to convince Menahem to return to his childhood Orthodoxy. He also promised to contact a wonder-working rabbi who worked miracles for women who could not bear children. (Since I had undergone a hysterectomy to remove a vaginal tumor in Eilat, we were childless.) This wonder-working rabbi was reputed to be able to restore my fertility! However, by the time the conversation ended, he was speaking softly and with genuine interest in and concern for us. When Menahem reminded him of his angry outburst and wish that he should be burnt up with the office, he responded with great conviction, in Yiddish, "But you are my brother!"

After a few years, the owner of our rented flat sold it to a young secular kibbutznik, Hovav, who for a while decided to continue our lease. He had no problems with our faith, as he professed to be without faith; we had several good-natured discussions with him. In our ninth year in the flat, he told us that he was intending to marry and that he and his fiancée were going to live in the flat. He generously gave us as much time as we needed to find another apartment, and invited us to the kibbutz where he had grown up for the wedding.

It was a lively affair, and we met Hovav's parents and some other German Jews who, like other members were ardent socialist Zionists who had immigrated to Palestine from Nazi Germany in the 1930s. We sat at their table as they reminisced in Hebrew and German about old times. There was a sadness in the nostalgia for their childhood, which had apparently been happy until the Nazi takeover. They reflected upon the idealistic dreams of their youth, when they had ardently believed that Zionist socialism and the common life were one answer to Jewish national homelessness and the recipe for curing social injustices.

But their children, like Hovav and his brother Gideon, while remaining in contact with the settlement, along with many other second and third generation people in the movement, were leaving the commune. Materially, the settlements had made tremendous advances from their primitive lifestyles of the 1930s. There was a certain touching sadness in their faces. They had succeeded against great odds in rehabilitating themselves, but were unable to transmit their ideals to many of their children, let alone to the larger Jewish community, which they had hoped would share their early vision and incorporate it within the mainstream of Israel.

By the end of 1986, we found another flat in the same neighborhood. We had not felt any excessive pressure in the previous building, which we had occupied for nine years. It had included a mixture of secular, traditional and Orthodox Jews, with several being Jews of Persian background. We assumed that the new flat would be a similar mix. It was not long before we learned that it was a mix indeed, but one that included some extreme Orthodox Jewish families, which could even be classified as ultra-Orthodox. One family was comprised of a zealous Swiss Jewish woman married to an intensely bitter Czech Jewish Holocaust survivor, with a large family of devout children. There was also an Orthodox American rabbi and his wife and an English Orthodox Jewish couple in the building.

The trouble began with a Gentile French tourist who was enlisted by a local Jewish evangelist from outside Jerusalem to distribute a special Hebrew edition of the Gospel of Matthew—presumably to individual Jews who, as stated in the preface: "In appreciation of this gift, I promise to read this booklet." The young Frenchman, who knew no Hebrew, decided that the best prospect of wide distribution was to slip copies into every letter box in the neighborhood. One can imagine the reaction of Jews, Orthodox and secular, who had allegedly promised to read a Gospel in appreciation of a gift they had never solicited.

We first learned about it from a neighbor, a very secular Jewish law student on the floor below us. She knocked on our door one evening and emotionally informed us that she was a firm believer in freedom of religion, but that mailbox distribution of Gospels was an insensitive invasion of privacy, especially among Orthodox Jews who were Holocaust survivors.

About the same time, Menahem received a letter addressed to the Alliance asking to be in touch with the organization as "newcomers." Although he was suspicious of the letter, especially the word "newcomers," he was not doing anything illegal, nor was the Alliance part of an underground movement. On the outside chance that it was a genuine request for contact, Menahem acknowledged the letter, enclosing a small Hebrew booklet published by the Alliance, "Messianic Jews: Who are They and What are They?" Two weeks later, photocopies of the letter and two pages from the booklet were posted on the bulletin board of our building and throughout the neighborhood on lampposts and other public areas warning that the Benhayims were dangerous missionaries and must be shunned. For several months, the posters were everywhere. The campaign had begun!

A sympathetic bank clerk we knew, as well as the wife of a Reform rabbi in our building, began tearing them down. A secular young neighbor reacted by scrawling on the bulletin board, "Enough of this incitement. Let it stop!" The campaign aroused the most intense hatred among the Orthodox Ashkenazi residents who expressed their hostility by cursing, encouraging their children to spit in our presence, threatening phone calls and fake warnings that a bomb had been placed in our car and that our flat would be set on fire.

Even more serious was the stalling of the elevator on the top floor when fanatics saw us entering the building. We had to walk up the five floors to our apartment, not to speak of the risk of elevator damage. It was obvious that they were trying to force us to leave. More tolerant neighbors, Middle Eastern Jews, were cautioned in our presence or in their homes to shun us as *meshumadim* ("apostates"). Pressure was placed upon them not even to respond to our *"Shalom!"* Nevertheless, the Middle Eastern Jewish neighbors remained civil and, to a certain degree, even friendly.

Unsigned notices were placed on the bulletin board in response to letters Menahem had written to the house committee. We were falsely accused of bribing children with sweets, making Gentiles out of Jews, "buying souls" and helping Jews to emigrate to "Christian" countries. When we attempted to respond to the false charges, our letters were torn down as soon as possible. Endeavors to address our adversaries in the building were met with slammed doors or angry words. The Orthodox American rabbi to whom Menahem appealed for a man-to-man talk turned on him with a wild, violent look. Raising his voice, he shouted, "I do not talk to traitors!"

The Reform rabbi on our floor, who surprisingly had good relations with one of the zealot families, was asked to try to moderate the campaign. He told Menahem, "I spoke to them and there's no use. They won't change their tone!" This sustained hatred continued for twelve years, although not quite as intensely after they realized that we were not going to leave.

A pleasant surprise came in the actions of a very pious Ashkenazi Israeli-born woman married to an Orthodox American Jewish immigrant. She remained friendly to me, and quite civil throughout the years, despite the pressure that we assumed was put on her. Her husband remained cool, but without the more rabid behavior of other Orthodox—usually Western—Jews.

When she suddenly became ill during this period and died, we were truly saddened. We did not attend the funeral, as we knew that the fanatics would be present and we wanted to spare the family should they make a scene at the graveside.

We nevertheless decided, with some apprehension, to visit the family during the *shivah,* the traditional seven-day mourning period. We brought a customary gift of food. To our relief, the husband received us politely and volunteered answers about the circumstances of his wife's sudden passing. Afterwards, his attitude towards us became much more positive.

Menahem retired in 1993, in order to turn over the Alliance work to a younger person who had grown up in Israel. Gershon Nerel had come to the country as a young man from Transylvania with his parents. He married Sara, a daughter of Bulgarian Jewish immigrant believers, Hayim and Rachel Haimoff (Bar David). They had raised a family of seven in Ramat Gan, and several of their children became part of a Messianic moshav (community settlement) in the vicinity of Jerusalem. Gershon and Sara joined the moshav, called Yad Hashmonah, and Gershon in time started work on a thesis in the framework of the Hebrew University on the subject of Messianic Jewish self-identity. On its completion, he was awarded a doctorate from the University.

After Menahem's retirement, we remained active in the Messianic community, as well as in a Messianic Assembly in Jerusalem. Menahem served in the Assembly as an elder for several years. We were also invited to speak at conferences and before groups of believers both in Israel and abroad, sometimes with people who were curious about the movement and not necessarily believers. Menahem was also able to devote more time to writing and lecturing about the Messianic Jewish movement. For eight years, he published an independent Hebrew periodical called *B'shuv* ("Return"), which aimed at strengthening the Jewish link to our faith and hope in the contemporary Israeli context.

The Hebrew name for our movement, *Yehudim Meshichiim*, is translated "Messianic Jews" but is used much more comprehensively in Israel than it is in the Diaspora, where it is applied to Jews who give strong emphasis to Jewish tradition. In Israel it embraces, in various degrees, Hebrew Christian "fundamentalists" and other evangelicals, as well as those who emphasize the links to more traditional Jewish life. In fact, as the movement grows, there will no doubt be a measure of stress, within Israel at least, over how Messianic believers define and practice their Jewish lifestyle and relate it to the many-sided character of modern Jewish life. This is an ongoing struggle in Israel in which we all take part.

It is significant that for many years there has been developing a distinctive Messianic music in Hebrew, focused on Scriptural texts but sometimes also with original lyrics. Many of the congregations will not use the older Hebrew hymnals, which contain mostly translations of Christian hymns and a few traditional Hebrew songs. There are other indigenous frameworks, including youth, family and golden age conferences under the auspices of *Keren Akhva Meshihit,* led by Victor Smadja, a pioneer in the Israeli Messianic movement since the 1950s. We believe that something authentically Israeli and Jewish is emerging from this encounter with Jewish life in the homeland—and one which will be able to reproduce and reinstate that genuine Jewish expression of Messianic faith that began in the first century.

COMING AND GOING IN THE
SHADOW OF ARMAGEDDON

Twelve years . . . fifty years . . . a thousand years. What are they in the life of a people with a story stretching back to the dawn of history? The psalmist and the apostle plainly teach that *"with the Lord one thousand years is as one day."* And lest we despair at the fewness and insignificance of the *"days of our years"* we are comforted by the thought that *"one day is also as a thousand years."* (Psalm 90:4, 10; 2 Peter 3:8)

One hesitates in summing up. We are all strangers and sojourners upon the earth, all moving along for shorter or longer stays at our various way stations in the wilderness of life. Now I can see something of how the Lord works in time, even if it is only a partial view, "as through a glass darkly."

> *Bless the Lord, O my soul, and forget not all his benefits, who forgives all your iniquity, who heals all your diseases, who redeems your life from the Pit. (Psalm 103:2-4)*

Neither Menahem nor I were spared trouble, anguish, pain or disappointments. God has brought us through them all. There's no perfection in this life and I don't expect to find it. In heaven with Yeshua we'll be in our final home. Then all the promises will be perfectly fulfilled.

Living in Israel, I can also see God's faithfulness, whose promises don't fail in earthly matters either. Through wars and rumors of war, terrorism and strife on every side, the whole world seems at times to be lining up against Israel, yet God remains faithful to the promises He made to our fathers. He remains the God of Abraham, Isaac and Jacob and of their descendants.

For us, the trials and tribulations we've endured are a miniature of God's dealings with the people of Israel. As Messianic Jews, we aren't recognized by the vast majority of our own people. Many think that we are unfaithful Israelites, or sometimes we're called "former Jews." Even in Israel, we experience the feeling of what it is to be a Jew in the world at large. The world is often unfriendly, indifferent, sometimes openly hostile. But we are assured that the Scriptures concerning Israel's national and spiritual salvation will be fulfilled in Israel's life as they are being fulfilled in ours.

Meanwhile, we pray, *"O that the salvation of Israel were come out of Zion. When God brings back the captives of His people, Jacob shall rejoice, and Israel shall be glad"* (Psalms 53:6, 14:7).

As this is being written, threats are once again being uttered against Israel in the councils of many nations, as in ancient times, and to the same effect: *"Come, and let us cut them off from being a nation, that the name of Israel may be no more in remembrance"* (Psalm 83:4).

Great powers contend with one another over Israel's fate. At times, the destiny of the world seems to hang in the balance.

Are we living on the eve of the Armageddon? Only God knows. But we do know that the shadow of Armageddon hangs over Israel continually. Whatever happens, God has His remnant in Israel, as among all peoples. Finally, we shall see that Israel will turn back to God and be reconciled to His Messiah Yeshua—whose very name means "Salvation" in the Hebrew tongue. *"And so all Israel shall be saved"* (Romans 11:26).

Eternity will break through again. The most glorious

events will take place. Joseph will again be reconciled with his estranged brethren.

When shall I reach that happy place
and be forever blessed?
When shall I see my Father's face
and in His bosom rest?

I am bound for the Promised Land
I am bound for the Promised Land
O who will come and go with me?
I am bound for the Promised Land.